To Liberty

To Thomas Jefferson who defined it

To Ayn Rand who lived it

To my father and all soldiers who have fought for it

Critical Mass:

Life, Liberty, and the Pursuit of Better Government

Critical Mass: Life, Liberty, and the Pursuit of Better Government

Published by Escot Innovations

For information:

sscottyapp@msn.com

ISBN: 0-9700374-0-6

Cover illustration 'Fusion Flag' by S. Scott Yapp

Table of Contents

.

Critical Mass

Chapter One

Prelude

A few years ago, I began to study the founding documents of our country. My research began because of my growing disappointment with our current crop of leaders. It culminated in the book you now hold.

From the very beginning, I was surprised at what I found in the Constitution, The Federalist Papers, and the other documents of America's creation. My purpose here is to convey my discoveries to the reader. I'm not a literary genius, but it is my hope that the message will outweigh the lack of eloquence of the messenger.

I know you have heard it before, but our country is at a crossroads. In one direction is a dark future, where the government is all-powerful, where individual rights have been replaced by the 'good of society', and where personal freedom, individuality, and innovation are suppressed. In the other direction, is a country with a small central government that respects the rights and individuality of its people, with clear simple laws, and no special interest groups helping to push through draconian laws.

Our founding fathers envisioned a government for the people, by the people, and of the people, but what we have is a government for the special interests, by the professional politicians, and of the lawyers. The laws have become so complex that it takes a lawyer to do anything from buying a home, to adopting a child, to even running for political office. A simple mathematical error on your tax forms and your life could be ruined. Our prisons are overflowing with people who have not hurt anyone (except maybe themselves), while rapists and murderers are set free to make room for them.

Over two hundred years ago, men of great vision and courage stood up and declared themselves free. "*Give me liberty or give me death*" said men like Patrick Henry. These men were willing to die for this thing they called liberty. They knew what it meant. After they had won the war for independence and freedom, they gathered in Philadelphia and wrote the Constitution for their new republic based on this principle of liberty. A rule book, so to speak, to guide the new republic on its way. They had lived under the kings' rule, and they wanted to limit the power of government, and recognize the ideals of natural rights.

So what happened to this limited government? What happened to the notion of live free or die?

Most people in this country would not support socialism. Yet we have allowed our leaders to herd us in that direction. One of the attributes of a socialistic society, is the notion that wealth must be divided up. What are low-income grants, earned income credits, and enterprise zones in poor neighborhoods if not dividing up the wealth? Don't get me wrong, I believe that we should help the poor, but not through the federal government. This should be done through personal donations, churches, and charities.

We have moved towards Karl Marx's twisted dreams with the notion that the needs of the many outweigh the needs of the few. This is a nice sound bite, but it is not what this country was founded on. We live in a country that was formed with individual rights in mind. Our forefathers came to this country, from societies that were completely oppressive of those that thought and lived differently from the 'official' way of life. Our Constitution put into place certain guaranties that this would not happen in America. From the separation of church and state to the freedom of assembly, they set into motion the freest society man has ever obtained. This country was the first formed on the premise that 'we the people' give the government its rights and not the other way around.

Almost every issue that confronts us today can be addressed by using the simple logic of our forefathers. The philosophical ground on which they stood we now call capitalism and liberty. By applying these moral principles to today's problems, we could solve many of them. Why then do we allow our leaders to chisel away at our Constitution? Why do we allow them to deny our natural rights?

A quick view of the issues that confront us will show how far we have strayed from the principles this country was founded on;

On education, our founding fathers were silent. That is because it was never their intention for the federal government to be involved. I've heard it said that the federal government is the reason that our schools are as good as they are. I contend that the teachers the students and the parents are what makes them at least what they are, but our students lag behind students of other countries in almost every area. Many of them must have metal detectors and law enforcement in an attempt to make them safer. They no longer can teach ethics or morality. The federal government's overstepping of their constitutional constraints by being involved at all in education is, I believe, at the root of the problem.

Our welfare system is a failure. We have now raised a generation of second class citizens who depend on the government for handouts. The 'great society' has bred an underclass with no skills, no initiative, and no work ethic. Meanwhile the rest of us must foot the bill.

Our military has fallen into the trap of being the world's police force. We maintain (at our expense) bases all over the world. Thomas Jefferson being the visionary that he was, warned us to stay out of the affairs of other countries, but those who continually espouse the 'good of society' have extended their 'vision' for our lives to the people of the world. Every rebellion or small war that breaks out is determined by our leaders to somehow affect us. Then we interfere, sometimes with disastrous results. A case in point is Bosnia. By taking away the Moslems ability to defend themselves (by putting in place a weapons embargo), we enabled the Serbs to overtake most of the land, build concentration camps, operate rape camps, and slaughter tens of thousands. Only when the images of human skeletons, dead children, and the horrors of Serbian aggression began to play out on the nightly news did our leaders try to undo what they had done. Then, at our expense, we moved in with our troops to defend the Moslems. If we had allowed them to arm themselves to begin with, we would never have had to put one American soldier into harm's way.

Our leaders have stifled innovation. From farm subsidies to the national endowment for the arts to a hundred other federal programs, they have set up rewards for failure. The farmers, artists, and others that are innovative are then put at a disadvantage because the failures still have the money to continue competing. If art cannot stand on its own in a free market, the artist needs to change professions. If a farmer loses money year after year while his neighbors are making it, he's doing something wrong and needs to make a change. We do not need to support them, because by doing so we are assuring that next year they will do things the same way and we will be supporting them year after year after year thereby not only rewarding failure, but also breeding it.

More and more of our rights have been taken away by this notion of 'the good of society'. Many people (and most of the politicians) believe that we must all live the way or lifestyle that they choose for us. What happened to freedom? In the name of 'the good of society' they have slowly whittled down the Constitution. From the right to bear arms to the freedom of speech our Constitution has been and is under attack. From extremist groups on both sides of the aisle have come attacks on our personal freedoms. From rightist extremists like the Christian coalition and the 'moral majority' (which is neither moral nor the majority, by the way) to the leftist extremists like NOW and Greenpeace have come pressure on lawmakers to write laws that affect you and me by limiting and eliminating some of our God given and constitutionally protected rights. All in the name of 'the good of society'.

Why do they do this? Is it the power over us they seek? Is there a monetary gain at stake? Do they look at us as children that they must look out for because we are too stupid to do it for ourselves? These are the questions that we should ask ourselves every time a new law is proposed.

Prelude

The question may arise; who is he to say what is wrong with our country, and how we should change it? I ask, whom better? I'm not a lawyer (that's a plus in my book). I'm not a politician. I'm not a Rhodes scholar. But I am an American, and that's enough credentials to let me speak my mind.

I've worked for a living all of my adult life. I've discussed politics with people from all walks of life, and many of the political elite who think that we average Americans don't know what's going on, are in for a big surprise. We do. We know that our leaders who pass law after law and policy after policy are spending <u>our</u> money every time they open their mouths. We should also know that we have the power to change it. However, what we don't know is when we'll hit critical mass. That's the point where we act to change it.

I think the time is now.

Chapter Two

Jefferson, The Constitution, and the Federalist papers

Many arguments about today's issues are about the Constitution and the intent of the Constitution. For instance, I've heard it said that there is no separation of church and state implied in the First Amendment. One televangelist in particular, who wants a fundamentalist society, cites laws made before the Constitution as proof that this nation was founded on Christianity. On gun control, politicians make arguments for and against, and argue about the intent of the Constitution. Who is right? How do we find out?

We do have an advantage here. It is quite possible to know the intent of the Constitution.

After the Constitution was written, the states had to ratify it. To drum up support James Madison, John Jay, and Alexander Hamilton wrote a series of articles in the newspapers explaining the document and answering the questions of the people. These articles are now collectively known as *The Federalist Papers.*

Before I began this book I had never read *The Federalist Papers*. They are mentioned only in passing in school textbooks. Now that I have read and studied them, I believe that they are some of the most important documents ever written. Thomas Jefferson wrote that the Federalist Papers were "*rarely declined or denied by any as evidence of the general opinion of those who framed and of those who accepted the Constitution of the United States, on questions as to its genuine meaning*". As I will show, our leaders have obviously never bothered to read them. What I have discovered in them has caused a change in the very core of my thinking. I have since disassociated myself from both major political parties. Even worse (actually, even better) I have realized that there is very little difference between the two. They are both wrong.

My original intent upon beginning this book was to be a voice of moderation in a time of excess. I had been in both of the major parties at one time or another, and considered myself to be a moderate independent. But as I read the documents from those great men who risked and gave all for what they believed, this book became something quite different. It became a journey of freedom and discovery for myself, and I began to realize for the first time what liberty truly means. I knew and felt in my heart what Patrick Henry meant when he uttered those immortal words; "*Give me liberty or give me death*".

In the following chapters I will refer to and quote *The Federalist Papers* many times. I have found them to be very enlightening and concise. They contain the best reference to our Constitution, the document that protects our freedom. I will also quote Thomas Jefferson, undoubtedly the philosopher from whom our freedom flows. I will start with a quick look at the Constitution.

The Constitution begins with the preamble;

"We the people of the United States, in order to form a more perfect union, establish justice, insure domestic tranquility, provide for the common defense, promote the general welfare, and secure the blessings of liberty to ourselves and our posterity, do ordain and establish this Constitution for the United States of America."

Before I continue, I feel that I must define *liberty,* since this is the subject of most of the Constitution and the Declaration of Independence. So in this context I feel that the original intent must be known. We can find it in Thomas Jefferson's definition of liberty;

"Of liberty I would say that, in the whole plenitude of its extent, it is unobstructed action according to our will. But rightful liberty is unobstructed action according to our will within limits drawn around us by the equal rights of others. I do not add 'within the limits of the law,' because law is often but the

tyrant's will, and is always so when it violates the right of an individual."

Jefferson continues;

"I would rather be exposed to the inconveniences attending too much liberty than to those attending too small a degree of it."

As I studied the Federalist Papers and other writings by our forefathers, I began to realize what they fought and died for. ***Liberty.*** We use this word and never really understand it. We throw around words like liberty and freedom and never ponder the meanings. In the first quote above, Jefferson tells us that liberty is our freedom to do what we choose as long as it doesn't take away anyone else's freedom. It also tells us that the law can be wrong, and is always so if it violates our rights. In the second quote he goes farther by saying that too much liberty is better than not enough liberty.

What does this mean in today's world? This means that many of our laws don't meet Jefferson's test for liberty.

If liberty is the freedom to do what we choose without infringing on another's freedom, then a crime with no victim is no crime. Jefferson again; *"Laws provide against injury from others, but not from ourselves."* This point is crucial to freedom, since many people want you live the way that they choose for you. Many people believe that they have been given the right to choose what's best for you. From sexuality to drugs to guns, they know what's best for all of us. But a strict adherence to the Constitution, and the liberty and freedom as designed by our forefathers, would keep the haters of freedom from taking ours away.

Unfortunately, our leaders have not adhered to the Constitution. Most of them probably have not read it and if they have that's even worse because that means they either don't understand it or that they knowingly have violated it. Almost every clause, every sentence has been subverted. It reminds me of the book, *Animal Farm*, in which the pigs, being the only animals that can read, interpret the laws to benefit themselves. Why do you think laws are written in legalspeak and hard to clearly understand? The Constitution was not written this way. For the most part it is clear and simple. Where it is not, we have the Federalist Papers to show us the original intent.

The Constitution is broken into sections and subsections, many of which the do-gooders have subverted or tried to subvert.

Article One deals with the legislature. Even though I think that term limits are a good idea, they would have to be voted in by Congress in general, and not by individual states as is being tried. Article One, section five, clause one states; "*Each house shall be the Judge of the Elections, Returns and Qualifications of its own members.*" As to the intent of this Jefferson said; *"[Can] the States... add any qualifications to those which the*

Constitution has prescribed for their members of Congress? Had the Constitution been silent, nobody can doubt but that the right to prescribe all the qualifications and disqualifications of those they would send to represent them would have belonged to the State. So also the Constitution might have prescribed the whole and excluded all others."

Our leaders have set up grants (can you say pork?) for science and arts (National Endowment for the Arts) but Article One, section eight clause eight only gave them the power; to *"Promote the Progress of science and useful arts, by securing limited times to authors and inventors the exclusive rights to their respective writings and discoveries."*

The President has sent our troops into harms way under the guise of 'peacekeeping' even though Article One, section eight, clause eleven, gives the power to Congress not the President *"To declare war, grant Letters of Marque and Reprisal..."*

The executive branch has ruled by regulation even though Article One, section eight, clause eighteen gives the legislature the power *"To make all Laws which shall be necessary and proper for carrying into Execution the foregoing Powers, and all other Powers vested by this Constitution in the Government of the United States, or in any Department or Officer thereof."*

The budget for the United States is complicated to say the least. The general summary is 380 pages, and experts have a hard time following it. I myself, being very good at math (I'm an engineer) can not follow the trails of deception. I don't think that the published budget, even if accurate, meets the requirements of Article One, section nine, clause seven;... *a regular statement and account of the receipts and expenditures will be published from time to time.*

Article Two deals with the executive branch. It is rather short and describes the election of the President and details his limited powers. It never describes or insinuates any law-making powers, yet our modern presidents have ruled by decree through department directives and executive orders. For example (and there are many to choose from), when the Department of Energy decided that toilets should only flush a certain amount of water and threatens toilet manufacturers with civil and criminal penalties, the executive branch has not only stepped on the rights of the free market, but have overstepped their constitutional authority. These government-approved toilets don't work very well by the way, what a surprise!

Article Three deals with the judicial branch. Article Three, section two, clause three is self explanatory and <u>very</u> clear; *The Trial of all Crimes, except in Cases of Impeachment, shall be by Jury.* It never says anything about trials without juries. Note the word *shall*. Our forefathers wanted it to be a big deal to hold a trial, and I think if we had stuck to that we wouldn't have over 2 million of our citizens in jail today.

Article Four deals with the states. In section one it reads; *Full Faith and Credit shall be given in each State to the public Acts, Records, and judicial Proceedings of every other State. And the Congress may by general Laws prescribe the Manner in which such Acts, Records and Proceedings shall be proved, and the Effect thereof.* When the voters of eight states including the state of California legalized marijuana for medicinal purposes, Congress not the justice department should "*prescribe the effect thereof.*" Yet the justice department will not recognize the voters' rights to overturn unjust laws.

Article Five is the amendment process.

Article Six is general provisions. In section one, clause two, it states; *This Constitution, and the Laws of the United States which shall be made in Pursuance thereof; and all Treaties made, or which shall be made, under the Authority of the United States, shall be the supreme Law of the Land; and the Judges in every State shall be bound thereby, any Thing in the Constitution or Laws of any State to the Contrary notwithstanding.* The encroachments on this are numerous, much too numerous to elaborate on in any one book, but I will give two good examples. At least two different bands have had albums (compact discs for the younger readers) that several localities have tried to ban. One of them, 2livecrew, produced a collection of sexually explicit songs entitled *As Nasty as they want to be.* The other, Body Count (a metal album with rapper

Ice T on vocals) was also explicit, but the objection was to a song called *Cop Killers.* This one I have personally heard, and found that what is expressed is political in nature, and is most definitely protected by the First Amendment (Freedom of speech and expression). These are also good examples of letting the free market take care such matters. If it hadn't been for all the attention given to 2livecrew, their record would have most likely have received very little recognition. A 'clean' version of the album entitled *As Clean as they want to be,* sold less than 100,000 copies where as the 'nasty' version went platinum very quickly after the controversy was played out in the courts and the media. The other example I will offer is the case of Paul Cohen who committed the dastardly crime of wearing a jacket with the slogan "F*** the Draft" on the back. He was arrested, tried, and convicted by a state court. Later the Supreme Court of the United States threw out the conviction, on First Amendment grounds. Both of these show not only violations of First Amendment rights, but also show that the local law enforcement also were in violation of Article Six.

Article Seven deals with the ratification process. The Constitution was ratified over 200 years ago.

Then begins the Amendments. There are a total of twenty-seven Amendments, the first ten being collectively known as the Bill of Rights. The First Amendment reads; *Congress shall make no law respecting an establishment of religion, or prohibiting the free exercise thereof; or abridging the freedom of speech, or of the press; or the right of the people peaceably to assemble, and to petition the Government for a redress of grievances.* The encroachments on these rights have been incredible. From the examples earlier, to prohibiting Native Americans from using peyote in their ceremonies, to keeping media out of war zones, to arresting and even shooting protesters, the First Amendment has been under attack for many years.

The Second Amendment states; *A well-regulated Militia, being necessary to the security of a free State, the right of the people to keep and bear Arms, shall not be infringed.* Many different interpretations of the Second Amendment have been expressed. To get to the true interpretation we must go to Thomas Jefferson; *"There are extraordinary situations which require extraordinary interposition. An exasperated people who feel that they possess power are not easily restrained within limits strictly regular." "It is the multitude which possess force, and wisdom must yield to that".* It must also be noted that the Bill of Rights is a list of the rights of the people. The right to bear arms is not the right of the militia, as some would have you believe, but rather; "*...the right of the people to keep and bear Arms, shall not be infringed".*

The Third Amendment has to do with the quartering of soldiers on private property, and the chapter entitled *"Jack-*

booted Thugs and Tyrants" expounds on military operations on American soil.

The Fourth Amendment states; *The right of the people to be secure in their persons, houses, papers, and effects, against unreasonable searches, and seizures, shall not be violated, and no Warrants shall issue, but upon probable cause, supported by Oath or affirmation, and particularly describing the place to be searched, and the persons or things to be seized.* This one has fallen victim to the so-called war on drugs. In the rush to stop drugs, never mind that this is a victimless non-crime, we now have no-knock busts and car searches (what happened to being secure in your effects?). We have seizures of property for use by law enforcement (conflict of interest), and we have a police force arming itself to the teeth and having either no time or no interest in fighting real crime where there is no monetary gain from the asset forfeiture laws.

The Fifth Amendment states among other things that *"...nor shall any person ...be deprived of life liberty or property without due process of law; nor shall private property be taken for public use without just compensation."* Note that nowhere does it authorize seized assets to be used by law enforcement. Seized assets should only ever be used to compensate victims. The only time property can be taken and used by the state is through the overused eminent domain laws and then only with just compensation. This is a highly important point, because otherwise, as our forefathers knew, the states power to seize and use becomes omnipotent, and reports from all over the country of police planting evidence and targeting more expensive cars and homes bears this out.

The Sixth Amendment states that in criminal prosecutions the accused has the right to be confronted by the witnesses against him. How then do witnesses testify wearing black hoods or behind screens? In the case of encroachment onto the government's Groom Lake facility near Rachel, Nevada (it's better known as Area 51), no testimony is required at all.

The Seventh Amendment is the right of trial by jury, and it makes reference to the rules of common law. One of the standards of common law is the right of jury nullification and most judges will not instruct jurors of this natural right. Jury nullification is the right of a juror to vote for a verdict of not guilty if that juror deems that a law is unjust, or that it is being unjustly applied to prosecute a defendant, even if that means a hung jury.

The Eighth Amendment states "*Excessive bail shall not be required, nor excessive fines imposed, nor cruel and unusual punishments inflicted*". What is taking someone's home, business, or vehicle away from them for victimless crimes called? I would call it an excessive fine. Also, our prisoners have been used as guinea pigs in all kinds of experiments including testing the effects of syphilis and LSD. I would call that cruel and unusual punishment.

The Ninth Amendment states that *"The enumeration in the constitution of certain rights shall not be construed to deny or disparage others retained by the people."* This is crucial for all Americans. Note that it does not say given to the people, but rather retained by the people. That is because your rights are God given or natural rights. We the people give the government its power; the government does not give us our rights, because they are already ours. The government can only recognize those rights, or in the case of the statists, try to trample those rights. Our founding fathers recognized this, and we should also. They are our rights, and these rights are not to be given away, the voters can not vote them away, they are still our rights, and we should fight to protect them if needed. Among these unenumerated rights are the right to control what you ingest into your own body, your right to open a business, your sexual rights, your right to travel freely, and your right to make a profit. There are many others, again too many to enumerate in a single book, but Jefferson did give us a rule of thumb; *"Laws provide against injury from others, but not from ourselves."* In other words, if there is no victim, there is no crime.

Amendment Ten has been completely disregarded by the federal government. It states; *"The powers not delegated to the*

United States by the Constitution, nor prohibited by it to the States, are reserved to the States respectively, or to the people." This amendment was meant to control the size of the federal government. It was to be small and with specific powers with all other functions to be handled by local and state government and not by central planning. In *The Federalist Papers*, the authors foresaw the federal government being smaller than any of the state governments. Jefferson knew from the historical models of Rome and ancient Greece that "*Government tends to grow."* In response to this the Tenth Amendment was added. But alas, our leaders have not learned the historical lessons, even the modern ones like the Soviets attempt at big centralized government. This unconstitutional power grab by the federal government will lead to our demise, if we do not soon reverse it.

Amendments Eleven through Twenty-seven have been added since the ratification of the Constitution, and I will briefly mention a few and the encroachment on them.

Amendment Fourteen Section one states in part *"No State shall make or enforce any law which shall abridge the privileges or immunities of citizens of the United States; nor shall any State deprive any person of life, liberty, or property, without the due process of law; nor deny to any person within it's jurisdiction the equal protection of the laws."* Let's just say this one is routinely disregarded. When police make traffic stops, issue no arrests, but seize money on the grounds that it might have been illegally obtained; they have not allowed due process. When New York City sells the cars of drunk drivers who have not yet been convicted, they are in violation of the Constitution. Anyone who can read this amendment and not see this important point of law is either a statist or a moron.

The Eighteenth Amendment was prohibition of alcohol, and fourteen years later it was repealed by the Twenty-first Amendment. I wonder how long it will be before our leaders and a majority of the people realize that the drug war is the very same exercise in futility?

The Twenty-seventh Amendment reads; *"No Law varying the compensation for the services of the Senators and Representatives, shall take effect, until an election of Representatives shall have intervened".* Our Congress just voted themselves a pay raise and called it a cost of living increase in order to circumvent this amendment. But an exact reading of it tells you that what they did is still unconstitutional. A rose by any other name…

As I will show, our leaders have tampered with and are in violation of the Constitution every time they are in session. They have deliberately trampled on our God-given and constitutional rights. Like the pigs in the book *Animal Farm* they have misinterpreted laws and wrote them in legalspeak (a language understood only by lawyers) in an effort to take away your rights. Why? Because they are tyrants, not unlike the one we rid ourselves of in 1776.

But don't take my word for it. Get copies of the Constitution and the Federalist Papers and read them for yourselves. They are both available on the Internet free of charge. Once you have, you'll know why the Department of Education doesn't want students to read them. If they did, our students would realize that the federal Department of Education is in itself unconstitutional.

Chapter Three

Freedom of Speech

When the First Amendment states our natural right to freedom of speech, what exactly does this mean? Freedom of speech was not intended to protect speech that most of us generally would approve of. There is no reason for our founding fathers to have protected widely accepted speech. It is there to protect Howard Stern, Bubba the Lovesponge, Louis Farrakhan, and all others whose speech may sometimes offend.

Does this mean we must provide them a forum? No, not at all. This simply means that they can speak their minds, not that they must. The free market is still the best and only good judge of ideas.

The statists would like us to believe that our freedom of speech was given to us by them and therefore can be regulated by them. It is no longer freedom of speech at that point. I feel compelled to point out again that our rights are natural rights, and not gifts from our leaders to be taken back or altered at their whim or the whim of the voters.

In the case of Howard Stern, and the lesser-known Bubba, many of their critics would like them taken off the air for the children's sake. We cannot, should not, and will not gear society for children. Maybe the reason for their 'concern' is that the statists want us to be like their children. Besides, every radio I have ever seen has a dial to switch stations and an off button. If you really don't like a radio or television program, use your free-market right to turn it off. Complaining to the FCC only serves to empower them to censor programming and your program may be next.

Another ploy they use is to call for the regulation of public airwaves. The Constitution does not differentiate between public and private. As long as speech does not deny another's equal rights, like yelling fire in a crowded theatre, then it is, and should be protected.

When it comes to Howard Stern, his ratings speak volumes. Many people like myself started listening to him after he stood up to the FCC. He has my admiration not only for standing up for our God-given, and constitutionally protected rights, but also for an entertaining and innovative show. The FCC has not only violated the Constitution by violating First Amendment rights, but has also violated the Fourteenth Amendment by levying fines without due process because they know that a trial could not be won against the "King of all Media", Howard Stern.

Freedom of speech is what separates us from all other nations. In Britain, the newspapers and radio stations are prohibited from printing or broadcasting stories that cast an unfavorable light on their government. This was one of the tyrannies that motivated our forefathers to seek independence from them.

Our system does not allow government approval or disapproval of our press. When the government coerces networks to plant anti-drug messages in television programs; they have violated the rights of freedom of the press. Freedom of the press not only means we are free to print any article without prior restraint, but it also means freedom from official coercion. By offering the networks cash incentives to plant anti-drug messages they have stepped out of the bounds of their constitutional authority. The drug problem is a political issue with a great number of dissenting opinions, and the government should not be paying networks to broadcast theirs in the form of propaganda.

What is freedom of expression? First it is artistic freedom. That is, we have the natural right to express ourselves through writing, music, arts, crafts, and other artistic means. The product of imaginations and minds can not be regulated. It is not only wrong for government to try, but it is physically impossible. What is in our minds is ours alone, and we should never be forced to share it or forced to keep our artistic expressions silent.

One must recognize that the Constitution spells this out, not to protect the Mozarts, the Rembrandts, or the Mark Twains. They are the popular and widely accepted artists. It is spelled out to protect the 2livecrews, the Maplethorpes, and the Rushdies. They are unpopular amongst many. If we allow only art that is widely accepted to be produced, art and therefore society itself will stagnate. The marketplace is the best judge. In a capitalistic society, artists are judged, and voted on by the free market.

Freedom of expression is also our monetary freedom to support the artists that we personally like. Again, we have a crucial point. The government should not force people to support art that is offensive to them. Since our perception of art differs radically from person to person, government can not fund art without offending someone. In a free society, government should not be funding art at all. It is the free market's job, not the government's. Remember that Article One, section eight clause eight only gave them the power to; *"Promote the Progress of science and useful arts, by securing limited times to authors and inventors the exclusive rights to their respective writings and discoveries."* That means that the federal government's only legitimate function in regards to the arts is to secure patents and copyrights, and to protect the artist's intellectual property. The National Endowment for the Arts is unconstitutional, and in a market where bandages on a canvas can sell, totally unnecessary and a waste of taxpayers money.

By public support of failing artists we are also keeping untalented or unpopular artists competing against the innovative artist. This flies in the face of the free market principles of our founding fathers. Our financial support is likened to our vote. In fact, it is our vote. We should be free to support those artists that we like, and by the same token, free not to support those we do not. This can not be achieved through government support of artists.

I object to my tax dollars being used to fund sewage on canvas. I object to money forcibly taken from the taxpayers to be used to pay for the trash that some would call art or music. If you like it, you buy it, but don't use the force of law to make the rest of us pay for it. It is unacceptable for government to pick our art and our music for us. Dismantle the National Endowment for the Arts, and end the dung war forever.

Chapter Four

Freedom of Religion

The very first phrase of the Bill of Rights is about the freedom of religion. Our founding fathers thought it was so important that they put it first. In order to understand why, we must look at the events surrounding the colonization and the eventual revolution of the New World.

This country was colonized by people that were, for one reason or another, considered as undesirables in Europe, Asia, and Africa. The immigrants that came over were religiously incompatible with the 'official' churches of Europe. Puritans, Quakers, and hundreds of religious groups risked all to come to these shores and worship as they pleased. Africans and Asians being of many different sects and religions were shanghaied by their own people and sold into servitude here. Such were the various religions started in the New World.

In the early part of the 1700's, the King, seeing that many denominations of Christianity, Judaism, and Islam had gained a foothold among the people, appointed Governors and legislatures to pass laws swearing all leaders to allegiance to the king and to Christ. Jefferson and the other founders were aware of this and had since seen religious intolerance here in the colonies.

Our forefathers were not silent on religion. They realized that even amongst themselves their religious beliefs varied. They had studied the history of religion and the impact that it had historically had on government.

Jefferson continually referred to the Creator. In the Declaration of Independence itself, he referred to God three times. He recognized that our rights are natural rights or God-given rights if you wish. In the Declaration he referred to these as unalienable rights, or rights that can not be taken away since they are endowed to us by the Creator.

So they, as Jefferson said, put a wall of separation between church and state. They knew that an individual's religious beliefs are personal, and that government should not be run by zealots. Historically they knew of the crusades, the inquisition, and of the burning of the Great Library. The loss of knowledge of the ancient world was profound and probably caused the dark ages to go on for centuries longer than it would have. The Salem witch trials had shown that zealotry could lead to the arbitrary murder of innocent people in the name of religion.

Our founding leaders knew that this could not be a normal way of life for a free people.

This wall of separation was to insure that these atrocities would never happen to Americans. They knew it was important to spell out not only our freedom of religion, but our freedom from religion as well.

Many people have a problem with this. The moralists believe that other people should live, as they themselves do, or as they try to say they do. From abortion to pornography to drugs, they have tried to legislate (force) their religious beliefs on to the rest of society. They find it difficult to separate their religious beliefs from their political beliefs.

This type of fundamentalism has no place in a government that respects the people's natural rights. Our religion, our beliefs, and our morality are our own. We should never try to force our personal ideas or ideals upon our fellow man, and we should reject those potential leaders who would force theirs upon us. For it is force that we are talking about. Government is the force of law, so any leader or potential leader who would misuse that force, by pushing their own personal agenda should be summarily voted out of office, or never elected in the first place.

Moral decisions belong in the hands and minds of the individual, not the government. The force of law should not be used to make decisions about what individuals can or can not do with their own bodies. This includes everything from drugs, to prostitution, to abortion. Morality is a choice that individuals must make for themselves. The government should have no say in these matters. It should only bring the force of law to bear on those who infringe on another's equal rights.

People will make their own decisions about morality, and government should respect this. If an individual makes an error in judgement, as long as that error has not infringed on another's equal rights, it is none of anyone else's business. Much of our morality and personality is framed by the errors we have made.

Today, there are well over 5,000 denominations of Christianity alive and well in the United States. Add to this the millions of Jews, Moslems, Hindus, Agnostics, Atheists, Buddhists, and others, and it's easy to see that our religious and moral views are as varied as we ourselves are. That is why we can't have prayer in public schools, for whose prayer will it be? If I were an atheist, why would I pray to God or Allah or Jehovah? On the same token, if I were Protestant, why would I pray to the Virgin Mary? The Bible itself teaches one that prayer is private. That's as it should be. Religion is a personal thing, and it needs to stay that way.

The Federalist Papers say very little about religion, and that is consistent with their beliefs that religion was a very personal matter. However, the fact that the First Amendment affirms the right of freedom of religion speaks volumes about just how important it was in their minds.

Jefferson however had much to say on the subject. He too thought that religion was a personal matter saying "*Our particular principles of religion are a subject of accountability to God alone. I inquire after no man's, and trouble none with mine.*" He also believed that Government should stay out of religion. *"I consider the government of the United States as interdicted by the Constitution from intermeddling with religious institutions, their doctrines, discipline, or exercises."*

The most surprising thing to some is that he also believed that religion should stay out of government. *"Whenever... preachers, instead of a lesson in religion, put [congregations] off with a discourse on the Copernican system, on chemical affinities, on the construction of government, or the characters or conduct of those administering it, it is a breach of contract, depriving their audience of the kind of service for which they are salaried, and giving them, instead of it, what they did not want, or, if wanted, would rather seek from better sources in that particular art of science."*

No discussion on Jefferson's view of religious freedom would be complete without his 'wall of separation' quote. "*Believing... that religion is a matter which lies solely between man and his God, that he owes account to none other for his faith or his worship, that the legitimate powers of government reach actions only, and not opinions, I contemplate with sovereign reverence that act of the whole American people which declared that their Legislature should 'make no law respecting an establishment of religion, or prohibiting the free exercise thereof,' thus building a wall of separation between Church and State."*

Go back to preaching Pat Robertson, Jerry Falwell, and all other zealots and moralists who would force their will and religious views on the American people. Better yet, I as did Thomas Jefferson, believe that those who can not separate their religion from their politics should do neither.

Chapter Five

Drugs

If you believe the polls taken in the US, then you find that one of the major concerns of the people is drug abuse. What exactly is the problem and what can we do to solve it? Is what we are doing working or are there better ways to do it? Is the problem with the drugs themselves, the addicts, the dealers, or the money associated with it? What were our Founding Fathers' views? These are the questions that need to be answered.

Lets start by defining the terminology. What is a drug? A drug is any substance that causes a change in the human body. A psychoactive drug causes a change in the brain function, thereby changing mood or behavior. Therapeutic drugs cause a change that is considered beneficial to the human body. An illegal drug is simply one that has been deemed unlawful by government. An addict is a person who can neither physically nor mentally function without a drug. A dealer is a person who has seen an opportunity to make a profit, and has no regard for any law banning the sale of certain drugs.

Now lets define the problems. We will start with the claim that drugs kill. This is true. Approximately 130,000 people die in the US each year as a direct result of taking drugs. The problem is that 125,000 of them die from legally prescribed drugs while only about 5,000 of the deaths are related to illegal drugs. Doctors, pharmacists, and patients all make mistakes contributing to this number. The violence associated with the money to obtain or distribute drugs claims 25,000 live, or nearly 5 times as many lives as the illegal drugs themselves (gangs fighting for turf, police raids, etc…). Additionally many of the deaths from illegal drugs occur because of poor quality control. Since there is no corporation with a quality control team to maintain a standard, many addicts die from impurities or from drugs that are too pure.

There is the claim that drugs cut down productivity on a national scale. How do groups like the ever-misleading Partnership for a Drug Free America achieve the figures they quote? First they start by assuming that drugs alone cause all loss in productivity, which is incorrect since most productivity loss is due to over-regulation by the government. Then they assume an optimum productivity and subtract the current productivity from that and viola' they have a productivity loss statistic to throw at us with no basis in reality. This is basically how they come up with many of the misleading statistics they cry about.

Next they claim that we must protect children from drugs. I ask, does the current system achieve this? The answer, of course, is no.

Recently it has been reported that highschool students can obtain heroin more easily than liquor. This makes perfect sense when you consider that alcohol is sold by legitimate businesses that operate according to regulations by the community. A drug dealer does not. Of course there are still those that say they want to save the children when they talk about banning drugs, and even going back to prohibition of alcohol.

Parents are responsible for rearing their own children. We can not expect government to legislate out of existence all things that we do not wish our children to see, to hear, or to experience. What is morality if not knowing the bad, but choosing the good? It does not 'take a village'. It takes individual and responsible adults who teach their children right from wrong. Our children will then make their own choices reaping the rewards for the correct ones, just as surely as they will suffer the consequences of the wrong ones. It is called life and we can not, nor should we want to shelter them from it.

In order to find a solution to the so-called drug war, we must look at it philosophically. I ask you, who owns your body and mind? You do, of course. If you own yourself, then who am I or anyone else to tell you what you can put in your own body? It then also stands to reason that if you allow government to dictate to you what substances that you can't take, then they can also use force and tell you what you must take. Immunizations, vitamin D in milk, irradiated fruit, yes they have started and where will it end? Add to this the fact that money, not reason, is the determining factor in making substances legal or illegal.

During the early part of this century, our government tried prohibition of alcohol. What happened then is a matter of public record. Turf battles over money and marketing, drive by shootings, law officers and politicians being bribed. Sound familiar? Did we learn nothing from this failure? Today we have police unwilling to fight the real crimes because they are too busy raising revenues through asset seizures of drug addicts and dealers. We have them planting evidence, stealing money from supposed suspects, and taking bribes, just as they were during prohibition.

During prohibition, a group of businesses that were heavy contributors to the politicians convinced them to make hemp illegal. Were they concerned about people? Not at all. The timber, cotton and related industries realized that hemp could be made into paper and clothing more cheaply than their own products. Hemp was made illegal because the politicians convinced the public that it was in their own best interest, when in reality, it was in the politician's best interest.

Since we are on the subject of hemp, lets look at it more

closely. Hemp is one the oldest known drugs, with usage going back at least 10,000 years. Very old hemp 'pipes' have been discovered worldwide. The American Indians knew of its properties, as have native cultures around the world. In the U.S. hemp has been used to make rope and has been used to treat illnesses. Our forefathers grew hemp. It was one of Thomas Jefferson's primary crops. The Declaration of Independence was written on paper made from it. In Europe they are now using it to make paper and clothing, as well as fuel and medicine. But in the U.S., the DEA has classified it as a dangerous drug, as "having no medicinal value". But we know this is a lie. It has been found in European studies to be useful in treating glaucoma, Aids, cancers, and various other illnesses. The FDA has approved studies in the U.S., but the DEA has refused to let the researchers buy or obtain the drugs necessary for the studies. The voters in at least eight states have voted overwhelmingly in favor of medical marijuana laws, but there again the DEA has threatened to arrest any doctor who prescribes it and any pharmacist who provides it. It is the third leading money crop in the United States providing many entrepreneurs with a large tax-free income. In fact, one California town has deputized the workers in a marijuana buyers club, so they can be exempt from federal prosecution. Keep in mind that all of this nonsense is about a non-addictive, non-lethal substance (Not one person has ever overdosed, it is medically impossible).

Drugs have now become the criminals favorite scapegoat. "I wouldn't have raped and killed her, your honor, but I was on drugs." What a load of malarkey. It used to be the devil made me do it. Now that judges and juries won't buy that anymore it's drugs, pornography, blackrage, abusive spouses, bad childhoods, low self-esteem, or any of a hundred other excuses. No one will assume responsibility for his or her own actions. Ayn Rand made a point of this in the novel *The Atlas Shrugged*, when talking about the people who said *"It's not my fault, you can't blame me."* This is the attitude of many people, and the sad thing is that judges and juries are buying it. If you commit a crime (see the definition in chapter 27), then you are responsible for it and should suffer the consequences. Any excuse is just an attempt to put the blame on someone or something other than where it belongs, on the perpetrator. We don't accept this excuse from drunk drivers, regardless of whether or not they are addicted, and we should not accept this excuse for any other crime.

The extreme profits made by the underground marketing of illegal drugs have now helped push the black-market economy of the US to be as big if not bigger than the 'legitimate' economy. Cocaine is worth 10 times more per ounce than gold. So are we on the gold standard or the white standard? The money involved has fueled the rise in gangs and other criminal activities in all of the US. Fully 60% of the people in jail are there on drug charges. So the answer to the 'drug related crime' problem does not lie in more prosecution. Remember that dealers operate with no regard for law. It's the money involved that they seek. The only way to curtail 'drug related violence' is to take the extreme profits out of the equation. But the drug war has had the opposite effect. By intercepting shipments, and prosecuting users and dealers, the price has gone up (remember the laws of supply and demand). In 1981 marijuana cost about 40-50 dollars an ounce. Today, depending on quality, the range is from 150-400 dollars an ounce.

The drugs that are easier to smuggle have enjoyed resurgence. Heroin use, which was on the decline for many years, has made a big comeback. Higher priced, but easier to conceal than marijuana, it has become the drug of choice for a new generation. In central Florida, it is the most widely used of all illegal drugs.

The cost of the drug war has been staggering. Law enforcement now spends more time and resources fighting marijuana than <u>all</u> violent crime combined. In fact the estimate is that since 1981 the drug war's total cost has been over 3 trillion dollars, well over half the national debt. Have we gotten our money's worth?

Add to this the cost to our freedom, and it becomes quite apparent that we have lost. We have lost not only the drug war, but also many of our individual rights in this futile battle. We now have officers of the law profiling on our roads, stopping cars, and confiscating cash. We have people losing homes, cars, and personal property that have not harmed another person. We have no knock, door busting arrests that sometimes have tragic results. We have government officials paying television networks to add propaganda to programs. We have courts releasing predators from prison to make room for addicts and dealers, building more prisons and wasting more tax dollars all the while. We have gangs fighting over the best dealing locations. We have searches and seizures in direct violation of constitutional law. The drug war has had a detrimental effect on the First, Second, Third, Fourth, Fifth, Sixth, Eighth, Ninth, and Tenth amendments. It has served the statists well in their bid to remove our constitutional protection of our rights.

The argument has been raised that if drugs were legal then we would have many more addicts. By looking at history, we can determine if this notion has merit. On the surface this idea sounds correct, but let's look at the figures. In 1914 there were no drug laws. The estimate is that 1.4 percent of the population were addicts. In 1969 during the time period of the hippie movement and its affection for sex, drugs, and rock-n-roll, 1.4 percent of the population were addicts. Today, after spending an estimated 3 trillion dollars of our tax money on the drug war, approximately 1.4 percent of the population are addicts. Science has suggested that the reasons for addiction are genetic. That is to say that some people are genetically predisposed to be addicted to something.

Studies have shown that only a small percentage of people who experiment with drugs become addicted. The people that are predisposed to addiction get hooked on drugs, alcohol (which I'm being rhetorical since alcohol is a drug), food, sex, or something else that is damaging to themselves. Since this is genetic, then the best place to tackle the problem is through science, not the penal system.

One other fact that the special interest groups that oppose legalization want you to overlook is the amount of people who die from legal drugs. Phen-fen caused much more heart damage than cocaine ever could. Viagra killed more men in its first 6 months than have ever been killed by marijuana. It has been estimated that legal drugs kill 25 times as many people as all illegal drugs combined.

The medical profession likes things the way they are. They are operating a government-sanctioned monopoly on drugs. I know when I need an antibiotic for a sinus infection, but I must first pay for a doctor to write a prescription. Why? Many say that they are the ones who are trained to take care of our health. But they make mistakes like the rest of us, killing tens of thousands each year. If I'm to be done in by a mistake, I would rather it be my own. Don't get me wrong, I'm not advocating a doctorless world, but rather one in which they do not have the power to override ones own personal choices by forcing us to use the medicine of their choice instead of being able to exercise our own judgement.

Drugs impair your ability to drive cars, trains, and operate equipment, this is a fact. One ad that I've seen tells you; "Don't believe people who tell you that marijuana doesn't kill." It then goes on to describe a train wreck that took the lives of several people, and tells us that the engineer tested positive for marijuana. What they don't tell you is that you can test positive for days after the effects have worn off, and that no one is advocating being able to drive or engineer a train while under the influence of any drug. We have drunk driving laws that test for blood alcohol levels, and are then used to prosecute people who drive while impaired. The fact that they drank is not what makes them criminals, but the fact that they operated a vehicle while impaired. I not only support such laws, but also would like to see similar laws put into effect for any drug that impairs your ability to operate a motor vehicle. An action is only criminal when it encroaches on another person's rights. By ingesting a drug (alcohol included), you may have harmed yourself. By getting behind the wheel impaired, you have then encroached on others rights to safe passage on the highway.

Jefferson of course agreed that people should control their

own bodies. "*Under the law of nature, all men are born free, every one comes into the world with a right to his own person, which includes the liberty of moving and using it at his own will. This is what is called personal liberty, and is given him by the Author of nature, because necessary for his own sustenance.*"

In conclusion, I would like to restate the reasoning for legalization. I defy anyone to come up with reasons not to legalize that stand up to the standards of freedom and liberty. (I say this with confidence because our founding visionaries were drug growers and users themselves). In the meantime here are the indisputable facts.

1.Over three trillion dollars ($3,000,000,000,000.00) spent on losing 'drug-war' (This has made the problem worse as previously explained).

2.Overcrowded prisons. 60% of all federal prisoners are there on drug charges; they have actually freed violent criminals like murderers and rapists to make room for drug addicts and dealers.

3.Adults have the natural right to decide what they put in their own bodies. (It's called liberty, you may have heard of it somewhere!)

4.It would take the excessive profits away from it. (How many boatloads of cocaine and heroin would be shipped here if there weren't big money to be made by doing it?)

5.No more excesses by the DEA (It wouldn't exist) and by local law enforcement. No more houses being busted into by mistake by law-enforcement with deadly results. No more seizures of innocent people's money and other property who must then prove that they weren't buying or selling drugs. Whatever happened to innocent until proven guilty?

6.It would bring back legal use of bigger bills like 500's and 1000's.They were dropped because of the drug war to make it harder to smuggle large amounts of cash, and so that government could more easily trace the flow of money. Can you say big brother?

7.It would free up the courts and law enforcement to go after the predators in our society. Police in 1999 spent more time going after marijuana growers, dealers, and users than they did on all violent crime combined. Of course this is because they can legally add money into their coffers from seized assets of addicts or dealers, while there is no monetary incentive to catch a rapist or a murderer. In Colorado there is a libertarian Sheriff who has virtually ended the drug war there. He was just reelected for a third term, despite stiff opposition. The people in his county have seen a dramatic drop in violent crime and an overwhelming 80% voted for him.

8.Tax cuts and revenue increases. By cutting out government departments at all levels (local, county, state, and federal) you can cut taxes. Then by applying an excise tax as there is on alcohol, revenue can be increased. One must just be careful not to set them so high that you encourage a black-market.

9.Drug safety. Right now there are no standards on heroin and a user can get 1% this time and 60% the next, and what the street level dealer cuts it with could be anything from coffee creamer to industrial cleaner.

10. A repeat from above, Liberty. (See definitions).

11. Just food for thought. If someone were to pay you $50,000 dollars a year to solve a problem, how hard would you work to solve the problem? Especially when you consider that the 'problem' has and most probably always will be a part of the reality that we live in. Sounds like a lucrative career doesn't it?

Chapter Six

Education

Who is responsible for your children? I have made it clear that I am responsible for my own, and I think most would feel that they are responsible for their own. But then, they vote for statists who believe that the government owns all children, and requires all people, even those who choose not to have them, to not only help pay to raise them, but to also live a lifestyle that's 'acceptable' for children.

The statists would have you believe that the education problem in the US is a result of too few taxes, and societal ills such as drugs and poverty. They also try to blame parents, pop culture, music, television, and their new favorite, Attention Deficit Disorder. What they don't want you to realize is that the state can never educate our children properly. More money hasn't solved the problems and as with most problems, big government solutions have just the opposite effect as intended.

When reading the Constitution, a fact becomes very apparent. There is no constitutional basis for the federal Department of Education. Our forefathers were all taught at home or at private schools. There were no public schools. Our education system during the 1800's was the envy of the world. Little red schoolhouses sprung up in every town and village. These were not public schools as such, but rather churches, farms, businesses, and local leaders help to set them up and they privately or locally ran them. Today our schools are the laughing stock of the world, with violence, illiteracy, and dropout rates on the rise. Teachers are underpaid, classrooms are lacking in supplies and computers, and the amount spent per student is increasing, with no positive results. Bureaucrats complain that the problem is too complex for us to understand, and what they need is more and more money to make their system work. They do not want to see the real problem: because they are the problem.

The number of privately educated and home schooled children in the US is on the rise. Violence, immorality, low test scores and objectionable curriculum have led many parents away from the public schools. Some of us, as parents, object to the socialistic teachings of anti-gun literature, Dare programs, or any one of a thousand personal issues that the public school system tries to ram down our children's throats. There are now even some high schools that your child can not graduate from without first performing community service. We complain that the schools are not teaching our kids ethics and morality, and not realizing that they can't.

The public school system can not teach morality or ethics for several reasons. First, the Constitution builds a wall of separation between church and state. The state can not teach ethics or morality without religion. Statists only know religion as a moral compass. They can not teach the morality of individuality, objectivism, capitalism, or even self-control. These internal moral compasses go against everything that the statists want your children to believe. They want your kids to believe that they live by the grace of the state, that the state knows better than the parents, that metal detectors at entrances are normal, that profits are a bad thing, that being different is okay as long as the differences are not better, that competition is bad, that mediocrity is good and the list of socialist and statist ideals go on and on.

Secondly, they can not teach morality or ethics, because they are void of these virtues. They highly praise programs such as D.A.R.E. (which like other programs has the opposite effect of what's intended), but then coerce parents into putting their children on Ritalin. They oppose vouchers by saying that it would take money away from public schools, and fail to acknowledge that it is our money to begin with, not theirs. Stealing is still stealing whether the money is being spent on children or on crack. They claim a shortage of qualified teachers, yet Bill Gates could not teach economics and even former Presidents could not teach political science. Many of us with real life experience who are considered as experts by the real world could not teach in our respective fields because we have not been socialistically indoctrinated with a liberal arts degree.

The Federalist Papers, the Constitution, and The Declaration of Independence are completely void of any reference to education. That is because it was never their intention for the federal government to be involved at all. This is one of those powers quite obviously that Amendment 10 is referring to when it states quite clearly; "*The powers not delegated to the United States by the Constitution, nor prohibited by it to the States are reserved to the States respectively, or to the people.*"

Some of our leaders are quite aware of the unconstitutionality of the federal Department of Education, but alas, they don't seem to care about the Constitution. The Republicans took control of Congress in 1994 and one of their promises was to eliminate the Department of Education. Now years later they have increased the department, and many of us who voted for them feel betrayed and dismayed by their lack of integrity. This along with other issues has led to a decline in their membership, and will eventually lead to their demise.

Chapter Seven

Pork Barrel Politics

Our government masters, just like the kings and queens of our feudal past, have every intention of retaining their power and status. They employ many methods of doing so, and one of their favorite ploys has always been to act as if they are being generous. I say act, because *how can you claim generosity when what you are doling out does not belong to you?* But our modern nobility has perfected this in the slop trough called pork barrel politics. "You vote for my program, and I'll vote for yours" has become the battle cry of our leaders. Meanwhile they use their pet projects to repay campaign contributors and political supporters.

In feudal times the nobles would ply their peasants with pageantry and public works like canals, wells, statues, and such. These generous 'gifts' would keep most of their subjects content with their leaders while the guillotine and the hangman's noose could keep small bands of malcontents quelled. Meanwhile, the nobility themselves lived lavish and carnal existences at the expense of their serfs. Grand cathedrals and such were built, while people starved.

The nobility demanded 1/3 or 33 percent of the peasant's harvests or wages to pay for the public works and to live the grand lifestyle that their subjects could only dream of. Today, our modern nobility demand 45 percent or almost half of our income, and they live a grand lifestyle that most taxpayers can only dream of. Keep in mind that unlike the working rich whose products and services we voluntarily buy; these parasites take our money forcibly in the form of taxes.

Today our new nobility plies us peasants with public works, pageantry, and anything that ***our*** money can buy them. They can vote themselves pay raises (and have many times), and they live lavish lifestyles at our expense. Instead of cathedrals they build museums to honor Lawrence Welk, or midnight basketball programs, or any one of thousands of other pet projects and paybacks for political favors. Each of the representatives tries to get as much federal money spent in his or her district as possible. Their buddies that helped to get them elected have plans to build all kinds of bridges, roads, libraries, and every other kind of project that they can dream of, and they would like to have somebody pay to build them. The problem is that under capitalism, these projects weren't built for a reason. *They are for one reason or another, not viable*. If they were they would have been built without taxpayer's money.

The part they won't admit to is that these projects are not only drains on taxpayer resources, but they are also unconstitutional. Many politicians will try to invoke the general welfare clause in the Constitution. The first paragraph of Article One section eight reads;

"The Congress shall have the power to lay and collect taxes, duties, imposts and excises, to pay the debts and provide for the common defense and general welfare of the United States; but all Duties, imposts and excises shall be uniform throughout the United States"

Note that Madison used the word general. This was meant to prohibit the federal government from using money for projects that would only benefit specific people or communities. This phrase does not mean, as the statists would have you believe, that the government has unlimited power to tax and spend. If this were true, the Constitution would be very short, for there would be no need to spell out the legitimate power of the federal government since this would make it omnipotent.

But the power is supposed to be limited. In Federalist Thirty-nine, James Madison wrote; *"... the proposed government cannot be deemed a national one; since its jurisdiction extends to certain enumerated objects only, and leaves to the several*

States a residuary and inviolable sovereignty over all other objects.

In Federalist Forty-one, he specifically addresses the clause. Although a complete reading of forty-one leaves the reader with no doubt of the intention, the following quote sums it up beautifully; *"For what purpose could the enumeration of particular powers be inserted if these and all others were meant to be included in the preceding general power? Nothing is more natural nor common that first to use a general phrase, and then to explain it by a recital of particulars."*

Madison goes on to say that if this clause was misinterpreted that it would mean that the government could destroy the freedom of the press, or the trial by jury. He called this idea absurd. Keep in mind that Madison wrote the Constitution. In Federalist Forty-four, he even talks about voting out those who misconstrue this very clause. So even in the first days of our republic, the statists were trying to misappropriate funds trying to use tax money for their own agendas.

In Federalist Forty-five he writes; *"The powers delegated by the proposed Constitution to the federal government are few and defined."* The examples go on and on, and so could I about the ideal of limited government. It is quite obvious that our forefathers believed that the federal government should be limited and small. So what happened?

The cost of our government masters bringing home the bacon is staggering. They use this staggering amount of cash that they have taken out of our pockets by doling it out to make maximum political hay. They have supporters who have voted for them that they want to pay back. They have financial supporters that they must pay back. Never mind if it's constitutional, they just cite the general welfare clause of the Constitution. But as I have shown, this is a deliberate misinterpretation of Article One section eight.

The majority of these pork-barrel projects, if actually needed, could be handled at the local level. If Denver Colorado needs a new stadium, it is up to Denver to build it. Hopefully, local politicians will get the business community to see the potential profits and build it using no taxpayer money. Recently, the city of Orlando Florida tried to put together a partnership of federal, state, county, and city funds (a nice way of saying taxes) to build a light rail system. What doomed this albatross was a combination of factors. First, the business community wasn't on board. But secondly, and more importantly, was the fact that a ride to International drive would have cost the rider (tourist) $1.00. The problem was that it would have cost the taxpayers $9.60 per rider. Now I myself should not care since I don't live in Orlando, right? Remember the partnership of funds? Every American taxpayer would have paid for this ball and chain.

It is completely unconstitutional for the taxpayers to be paying for local projects at the federal level. When things go wrong as in the examples above, the blame can be spread out and watered down by the politicians. But when these proposals are handled at the local level, the taxpayers best interests are more likely to be served. In the Orlando example, the final decision not to build was at the local level after an anti-tax group called Ax-the-Tax got involved and put pressure on the local officials to stop the project. Unfortunately, millions of taxpayer dollars (at least 45 million!) had already been wasted on studies, plans, seminars, consultants, bureaucrats dining each other etc. etc. It must also be noted that the statist politicians that tried to get this project built, and the liberal media types that support them are still crying about it in the press. They still try to say that they knew what was best for us and that the taxpayers should have just shut up and let them build it. They now are predicting doom and gloom for commuters in central Florida. This is typical behavior for our modern royalty.

Jefferson knew the problem with using public money for improvements as is evidenced by the following quote; *"You will begin by only appropriating the surplus of the post office revenues; but the other revenues will soon be called into their aid, and it will be a source of eternal scramble among the members, who can get the most money wasted in their State;*

and they will always get most who are meanest". Sound familiar?

It is my contention that if you follow the money trail from these projects, it leads to the politician's base of support, making a circle back to the politician in the form of campaign funds or even bribes.

One must remember when considering the money spent on these local projects, that it doesn't matter if we approve of the project or not. If the source of funds is from the federal government, it is unconstitutional and unwise for the reasons that have been stated. It is just as wrong for federal taxes to pay for a swimming pool in Houston Texas, as it is for them to fund an artist putting a cross in a jar of urine and calling it Piss Christ. I am offended by both.

Just by getting rid of all of these pork barrel projects, the income tax could be lowered or even eliminated. If cities need swimming pools, bridges, municipal buildings, or any other physical improvement, the cities need to pay for them. If they can not afford them, then they should not be built. If improvements like these are truly needed, private donors and corporations will build them. Stadiums, properly built and operated, make money and are best left to private entities to build. Don't force 8 dollar-an-hour workers to pay for improvements that will mainly benefit politicians and their upper-class supporters.

Remember, even though some of these projects sound like good ideas, and maybe some of them are; the Constitution prohibits the federal government from being involved in them at all. These are local issues that should be addressed at a local level.

These projects do serve to get the leaders good press. How good our leaders are! They have built a new library, or they have solved some fitful problem. How generous and beneficial they have been to us! Long live our government masters, for they are benevolent and beneficial to our common good. The press can be reeled in hook, line, and sinker by our parasitical leaders. Sadly enough, many of the people are taken in as well.

Chapter Eight

Corporate Welfare

Welfare reform has been touted as a big issue by the Republican flavored Socialists. They want to limit the time that people can be unconstitutionally on the federal dole. But what they don't want to discuss at all is the welfare they give their big business donors. It's a taxpayer funded, unconstitutional, and unwise thing that we call corporate welfare.

Big companies, little companies, mid-sized companies, it doesn't matter. Our tax and spend masters will hand them money to try to further their own agendas. Never mind that it's unconstitutional, never mind that it's anti-freemarket, never mind that the money is coming primarily out of middle class pockets, they will help out the needy (uncompetitive) company, or whoever has donated the most money, or kissed the most political butt.

Corporate welfare comes in many shapes and sizes. One of the favorite ploys to make it palatable to the American people is to say that it will create jobs. Pepsi-cola was given cash to expand its market in the Far East and thereby create jobs. It worked! Their market share in the Far East went up, and jobs were created. Unfortunately, *none of the jobs were in the US.* This means, they took hard-earned money out of American's pockets and put it into the pockets of foreigners. Is this what good government should do?

A look at the federal budget shows these are not isolated abuses of tax monies, but an everyday occurrence for our modern government masters. They always have some seemingly well-meaning reasons for their plying of the elite businessmen with more cash (keep in mind that it is *our* cash). In the name of creating jobs, creating trade, environmental consciousness, or whatever they can dream up, they spend our money by the billions.

Some of the more noteworthy recipients during the 90's were; Gallo Wines over $5,000,000. Sunkist nearly $10,000,000. Welches over $1,000,000... the list goes on and on and reads like a who's who of the fortune 500. Keep in mind that many of these are foreign and international companies.

Most of the recipients of corporate welfare could well afford to do whatever it is our government masters are paying them to do anyway. So why haven't they? Most of these schemes end up backfiring, as do most big government programs. These companies have not done these things on their own, because it is not in their best interests to do so. If it is not in their best interest, then it is also not in the best interest of the free market or of the taxpayer.

Now, let's make sure I got this right. First, they take money from me, a factory worker for a large company, at gunpoint I might add, since they will jail me if I do not pay my taxes. Then, they give it to the big wigs, maybe even the owners of the company I work for. The big money men then finance the campaigns of the people who have transferred my money to them and continually vote to take away more of my rights. Something smells really bad. Really, really, bad.

In many ways, corporate welfare is much worse than its public counterpart. These companies must compete against others to gain their profits. If the government is helping some of them, it is throwing off the balance of the free market. The biggest objection to it though must be on purely political grounds. The companies that lobby and support the politician's campaigns should not be able to walk away with millions of our tax dollars. This is absolutely a conflict of interest and a system ripe for abuse. Here again, by following the money trail, you will find that the recipients of corporate welfare are part of the base of monetary support for the campaigns of the politicians.

If a company can not compete with its products on its own merits, without tax money given to them by our elected royalty, then they should go the way of many others before them; into bankruptcy and oblivion.

Chapter Nine

The Politics of Crisis

Everything that happens today is deemed a crisis by our leaders or by the 'experts'. Drugs are a crisis, no matter that they have been around since the earliest recorded history, and the addiction rate is the same today as a hundred years ago. It is still a crisis. Why is this? What do the experts and the politicians hope to gain by scaring the public into believing that they are in some way in imminent danger?

By working people into a frenzy over some problem be it real or imagined, the politician or 'expert' is trying to gain or retain power, or gain, retain, or increase public funding for their own personal agendas. They want us to believe that this problem is a dire emergency and only they can solve it by their own methods.

Of course, we are just as much to blame for this since we believe these liars to begin with. Add to this the fact that we expect government to fix all of our problems real or perceived, and it's easy to see how our modern masters can exploit us.

The news media also plays into their hands. Crisis sells. Viewers increase during crisis. Look at CNN's viewership increase during the Gulf War. A real crisis surely increases their market share, so getting people to believe that there is some sort of crisis will do the same.

Our modern masters have perfected the game of crisis. No matter what the issue, it becomes a crisis in their minds, and they work very hard at making it a crisis in ours. They will pound on podiums on the evening news, and hold as many press conferences as it takes to get the public in the frenzy that they need to get their legislation passed.

If they are to be believed we might as well just kill ourselves and avoid the pending disasters. Just in the last few years we have been warned of the following crisis;

Y2K crisis

Illegal drugs crisis

Legal drugs crisis

HMO's crisis

Healthcare crisis

Doctors errors crisis

Campaign financing crisis

Education crisis

Education funding crisis

Teacher shortage crisis

Illegal immigrant crisis

Global warming crisis

Global cooling crisis

Polar cap melting crisis

Volcanic activity crisis

Overfished ocean crisis

Homeless crisis

Airline safety crisis

Obesity crisis

Loss of family values crisis

Morality crisis

Poverty crisis

Divorce crisis

Whitehouse intern crisis

Militia crisis

Gun proliferation crisis

Assault weapon crisis

School shooting crisis

Nuclear material crisis

Waste management crisis

Disappearing rainforest crisis

Blood shortage crisis

Military readiness crisis

Bosnian Crisis

Kosovo Crisis

Mideast peace plan crisis

Colombian Drug Crisis

Mexican Drug Crisis

We have perceived crisis and epidemics on just about every subject. Some of these are real problems, but government can not solve all of the problems of mankind. The more we ask government to do, the more rights they will take away. I believe that John F. Kennedy was wrong when he said *"Ask not what your country can do for you, but ask what you can do for your country."* The quote should have been *"Ask not what your country can do for you, but ask what you can do for yourselves."* We must solve many of these problems ourselves, or let the free market solve them in its own way. The politics of crisis has become one of the favorite tools of the statists to remain in power. One must take care not to join these choruses of doomsayers, and look past their rhetoric and see their lust for power and control of all aspects of our lives.

Chapter Ten

Who's in charge?

Layer upon layer of bureaucrats; that is what faces any citizen who has to have any dealings with the federal government. Which, by the way, is every one of us. It seems that nothing can be accomplished without some bureaucrat sticking their nose in your business and telling you how you must do it. There are fourteen different departments with law enforcement duties, a dozen dealing with American Indians, and thousands of bureaucrats living off the wages of people who actually produce something.

The joke has been made that Uncle Sam will tell you which hand to wipe with, and this is not too far fetched because he already tells you how much water your new toilet can flush. Yes that's correct, your new toilet can flush no more than 1.6 gallons of water, and by passing such an intrusive and stupid regulation, the laws of the free market dictate that a black market in toilets must be created, and of course it has. Toilets are now one of the biggest smuggled items into the US, and private designers will build illegal crappers for those with enough money to pay for them. The worst part of this regulation is that no elected official ever voted it in. It was accomplished through the executive branch, which is a violation of the Constitution. Articles One, Two, and Three, clearly separate the legislative, executive, and judicial branches. Jefferson said on this subject; *"It was fundamentally wrong to submit freemen to laws made by officers of the Executive."*

Various branches of the federal government routinely make regulations, collect fines and penalties, and force individuals and businesses to jump through various legal hoops, all in violation of constitutional law.

From the EEOC to the ATF to the FCC and every other combination of letters imaginable, bureaucrats now try to control all aspects of modern life. If you don't hire enough minorities, if you cut a shotgun's barrel off too short, if you don't run enough public service adds, or if you build a good-flushing toilet, expect a visit by governmental parasites, who will, for a fee of course, absolve you of your sins. Maybe if you're really bad and do something like provide marijuana for Aids patients, they will seize your assets and throw you in jail, even though the state you live in has legalized it.

This is just the tip of the iceberg. Through executive orders, modern presidents, especially Bill Clinton, have ruled by decree just as did the tyrants that we rid ourselves of over two centuries ago.

Recently, he announced that if the gun manufacturers did not settle the lawsuits with the cities and put in place several concessions, that HUD would join the lawsuits. His spokesman said this was because the Republican Congress was too slow to act on gun control. This is pure tyranny, as well as unconstitutional. Congress, not the President, has the power to enact laws. But they don't, as Slick Willy knows, have the authority to enact laws that violate the Second Amendment.

His departments have repeatedly tried to push through regulations like the banking 'know your customer' regulation that would have made all Americans suspects if they made any unusual deposits or withdrawals from their banks. Congress, after being made aware of this by their constituents, passed a law forbidding it. Now the banking regulators say even though that they could not pass an official regulation, that they want to see every bank employing these tactics, and will inspect banks that do not more carefully. This is legislating from the executive branch, and not only is it unconstitutional, but it is a form of tyranny.

Example after example of the executive branch unconstitutionally legislating could be cited here. They call such laws regulations, but sewage by any other name would still smell like, and be, sewage.

The Constitution sets out the separation of powers, but the government disregards it with impunity. One intrusion by government into the lives of its citizens is usually followed by another. Madison knew this and wrote in Federalist Forty-four; *"They have seen, too, that one legislative interference is but the first link of a long chain of repetitions, every subsequent interference being naturally produced by the effect of the preceding"*.

By eliminating some of these departments, especially the ones that overlap, and combining others like the various law enforcement entities, we could eliminate a great deal of government spending, and therefore lower tax rates.

But our modern masters like to rule by decree and regulation. They call it public policy, as if the public has any say in it at all. Ask the voters of the western states that voted to legalize marijuana for medicinal purposes if they have a say in public policy. Even when the voters overturn stupid regulations, our government masters decide they know what's best for us. This is the very definition of tyranny.

But no matter how loud or how long the statists try to tell us that the government is omnipotent, it will never be true as long as there are freedom-loving Americans who know their Constitution.

Chapter 11

Chapter Eleven

Justice

How much justice can you afford? Are jurors being fully informed of their rights as jurors? How can we insure that no one is jailed for crimes they didn't commit? Most importantly, how can we reduce crime without infringing on people's rights?

The price of justice seems to be going up and up. Lawyers charging by the minute, complex laws and regulations that create need for more lawyers, and personal freedoms taken away all in the name of justice. To understand justice, we must first know what it means.

Justice is the application of legal force to protect, compensate, or retaliate on behalf of a victim or victims, against a perpetrator or perpetrators.

Justice is taking back someone's property that was wrongfully taken from him or her. Justice is not taking away someone's property because we don't approve of what they do for a living.

Justice is putting someone to death who has killed another human being in cold blood. Justice is not taking away someone's liberty because they put something into their body that we don't approve of.

Justice is incarcerating those who prey on others. Justice is not prosecuting those who have not infringed on another's equal rights in the name of ' the good of society'.

Jefferson had a lot to say on the subject, my favorite quote being; *"Law is often but the tyrant's will, and always so when it violates the right of an individual."* He goes on to say; *"The sword of the law should never fall but on those whose guilt is so apparent as to be pronounced by their friends as well as foes."*

Jurors are not being fully informed of their rights. If a juror feels that a law is either unjust, or is being applied unjustly, then that juror has the right and duty to find the person not guilty. Jury nullification is a long established right and a natural right. I say natural right, because this comes from a person's own sense of justice and morality, which of course is in the person's own mind. The problem is that juries are not being informed of these rights, in fact many tyrant judges ban even the mentioning of these rights. Some judges have even tried to eliminate the secrecy of jury deliberations to prosecute jurors that exercise this right.

Everyone has read about police planting evidence, prosecutors leaving out details that would have cleared someone of a crime, and all sorts of misdeeds committed by individuals within our judicial system. From Miami to Los Angeles it seems that no police department or prosecutors office is immune from this. How can we insure this does not happen?

This problem has a very simple answer. If any official is found guilty of manufacturing, planting, lying, or omitting evidence that would have cleared a person that was found guilty and sentenced, then that official must serve that sentence up to and including the death penalty. This would make any police officer, prosecutor, or investigator, think twice before creating a miscarriage of justice.

The other common sense approach is to forbid police departments from using or obtaining any seized assets. It is clearly a conflict of interest to have arresting officers profiting directly or indirectly from the seized assets of criminals. By allowing this we encourage police to investigate certain crimes, and not investigate others. As has already been stated, investigation and prosecution of marijuana crimes now use up more of our law enforcement time and money than all violent crime put together. It also causes many miscarriages of justice since many police officers have now been found guilty of planting drugs in suspects' cars so they could confiscate them, sell them, and use the proceeds to pay for things like seminars in Hawaii.

A proper reading of the Fifth Amendment will tell you that what they are doing is unlawful. It says in part *"...nor be deprived of life, liberty, or property, without due process of law; nor shall private property be taken for public use without just compensation."* Our modern masters are quite aware of this, and now use the ploy of charging the property they want to seize with a crime. It should be quite obvious that what they are doing is wrong, unlawful, and the acts of tyrants.

How do we reduce crime without trampling on the rights of the individual? Legality in America today has no philosophical basis. Our modern masters rule by decree instead of logic. What is legal should be easy to determine, but our leaders have made sure that it is not. Laws should be clear, simple, and have two essential elements. A law should be able to identify a perpetrator and a clear victim. Society can be neither of these. Only specific individuals or entities can be either.

By misusing the force of law, and attempting to uphold personal views of morality as we do against drug users and sellers, prostitutes, gamblers, and nude dancers, to name a few, we actually are causing disrespect for the law. People who have not victimized any other individuals but are prosecuted anyway will grow not only to disrespect the law, but they eventually disregard it completely.

In recent years because of so many bad decisions by lawmakers and bureaucrats, our government has resorted to passing laws exempting its own members from prosecution or lawsuit. In this case the victim has no recourse but to sue the entire government, instead of the actual perpetrator. These protection laws, such as citizens not being able to sue a bureaucrat over a decision that costs a person their life, should be banned. An example of this is the children that were killed because a decision was made to make it a crime to disconnect air bags. Now, it's a crime not to. Talk about arbitrary law! Never mind that these are regulations from the executive branch, a clear usurpation of the Constitution.

This is part of what we objected to about King George and his henchmen. We objected that his troops and his governors were immune to prosecution and that laws were arbitrary. Read the Declaration of Independence. Many of the complaints we had about the tyrant are the same complaints we can lodge against our modern tyrants.

Chapter Twelve

Sexuality

Governments long have tried to pry into the bedrooms of the people. From the medieval practice of nobility sleeping with peasant girls on their wedding nights (many grooms were forced to watch their brides raped by the local baron), to our modern government masters trying to stifle any sexual deviation, leaders have always tried to force their own sexuality upon the common people.

Our founding fathers were silent about sexuality, and rightfully so. They assumed that sex was a private matter between adults. But our modern masters wish to make all things, even our sexuality a matter of public concern.

Fundamentalists call for a return to values, and I agree. We need a return to when matters of your private sexuality were just that; private. The fundamentalists however, are trying to be revisionists by saying somehow that people are more immoral now. We know from a study of history that this is not true.

From the very beginning of our country, there are historical accounts of affairs, gays in the military, congressional as well as Whitehouse bedroom antics, and all sort of sexual games being played. From George Washington to our present leaders, mistresses and rumors of mistresses have abounded. It is human nature, and only our own internal compass, our own morality, can lead us to be moral. No law or regulation has ever, nor will it ever, keep consenting adults from having sex.

Prostitution has been called the world's oldest profession, and I am inclined to agree with that statement. When they stoned women for it, it did not stop. When they burned them at the stake, it did not stop. Today, they jail them, and it does not stop. Why is this?

I think that Jefferson gave us the reason when he said that a crime with no victim, is not a crime. He also said that a law that attempts to protect us from ourselves is merely the tyrant's will. When consenting adults have sex, it may be immoral, but remember that morality is our own personal compass, and can not be forced onto others. It may be offensive, but being offensive is not a crime, since different things offend each of us. Crime can not be arbitrary; it must be able to be defined clearly with a perpetrator and a victim. Since prostitution has neither, in a free society it can not be a crime. It may shock your sense of morality, but you can not legislate morality since morality comes from within each individual.

If consenting adults share a room together, it is none of our business what they do in that room. Any attempt to invade the sanctity of the private bedroom is voyeuristic at best.

There have been gays around since the beginning of time. For most of history they have chosen to be in the closet to avoid the moralists' intolerance of them. I am not gay, but I do not care if someone else is. It is truly none of my business and it does not affect my opinion of them at all. However I do think that sexual behavior between people, be it heterosexual behavior, or homosexual behavior, is best pursued in private.

As much as I dislike the President's policies, his wife's proposals, and just about everything associated with Bill Clinton, his sex life is his own business. Monica Lewinsky was a consenting adult, and I do not care what they did, why they did it, or how many times they did it. Many have declared this a national disgrace, and I agree. It is a national disgrace that anyone should be able to even ask about his sexuality. I would have even cheered for the man if he would only had told them that it was none of their damned business. The only person who has any cause for concern is his wife.

For all the many reasons that Congress could have impeached Bill Clinton, they chose sexual deviation. Of course we know that many of them are guilty of the very same indiscretions. Some say it wasn't about sex, that it was about lying, but it was about lying about sex. Most of us, male and female, have lied about sex before. I think Farrah Fawcett told me this once while I was cooking her breakfast. I don't condone lying, but at one time or another, everyone does it. There are certain things that should remain private, and our sexuality is one of them.

My body belongs to me, and yours belongs to you. Consenting adults should be able to do with theirs what ever they want in private, and for whatever reasons they happen to have. It is none of anyone else's business if they are of the same sex, if money is exchanged, or anything about their encounter. Private moments are just that and we certainly don't need our obviously immoral leaders telling us how we should behave in private.

Chapter 13

War on Morality

Our founding fathers had a sense of morality that was based on more than religion. It had a philosophical base as well. From seeing capitalism as a virtue, to liberty, to the very natural rights espoused so well in the Declaration of Independence and the Constitution, they attempted to build the most moral society the world has ever known. What has happened to that morality?

Their sense of morality had absolutes, but our modern leaders try to tell us there are none. They wished for people to develop their own sense of morals, where our modern masters wish to tell us what ours must be.

There are moral absolutes. It is wrong to steal. Whether or not the stolen loot is used to by crack, or to buy food, it is still wrong. Whether the majority has voted to take money away from you, or a small minority has decided to relieve you of the fruits of your labor, it is still wrong.

This is the inherent flaw in the income tax. It makes stealing okay in the minds of the people, and is in actuality an assault on morality. For most of this country's existence we did not have this immoral theft of property, but the statists brought it into full swing during the Second World War, and the thieving politicians decided they couldn't do without it after the war was over.

It is absolutely wrong to take liberty away from those who have not infringed upon the rights of another, but in the name of 'the good of society' we lock up addicts, prostitutes, and gamblers. The Bible thumping moralists should remember how Jesus would have treated these people, and did treat them. But go ahead and stone them; the law of man is on your side.

The real fight for morality, the one that the politicians and the so-called moral leaders are waging against the people is their attempt to change our economic system from the moral system of capitalism to the immoral and evil system of socialism.

In our schools they are teaching Karl Marx and altruism, instead of Adam Smith and capitalism. In our churches they are teaching self-sacrifice and intolerance, instead of self-reliance and love. In our homes we are teaching our kids to loathe guns and hate competition, instead of the duty of free people to be armed and vigilant, and the virtue of working, and yes competing, for the brass ring.

Capitalism is a virtue. There are many voices, yes socialist voices, out there screaming about profits and the rich getting richer. You've heard these people, perhaps you are one of these people, that think that greed and profits are bad. The problem is that greed is human nature, and profit is the only reason that innovators and entrepreneurs try out new ideas or products. These two virtues, profit and greed, are what has made America the economic powerhouse that it is.

The rich are getting richer, that is a fact. But under capitalism, the poor are getting richer too. Look at the progress the world has made since the inception of this country and the capitalism it brought to bear on the world. There is no denying that the big capitalists like Rockefeller, Ford, Gates, Walton, and thousands of others some would now vilify, have made a tremendous contribution to the way of life that the free world now enjoys. Anyone who tries to downplay the importance of capitalism to the progress of society is a revisionist, and not worthy of our attention. It is the virtue of self-reliance and the desire to better one's self, which has led us to the prosperity that all Americans, rich and poor alike now enjoy.

There are those who wish you to believe that the poor have not enjoyed the benefits of this capitalistic prosperity. But even those to whom we refer to as poor still have the basic amenities of life, unlike the poor in some of the dictatorial and socialist countries that exist in this world. The difference is that in this country, through hard work, perseverance, and better ideas, capitalism gives us all a chance to succeed, to change our perceived station in life. This is the moral value we should all cherish.

My question to all socialists is this; How is it moral to steal from one man to give to another? It is still theft. Capitalism is the most moral system ever devised because it rewards those who will work and innovate, without punishing anyone. No one under a capitalistic system loses anything by force. No other system can make this claim.

It is also moral because it allows people to rise above any societal station, and does not assign such to anyone. Every member of a capitalistic system has the equal opportunity to pick themselves up by their bootstraps. The great thing is that by their hard work and innovation, the whole of society benefits.

Under socialism, innovation is suppressed because no one will innovate simply for the good of others. The altruists would like you to believe that this is a character flaw of humans. The truth is that this notion of greed is a virtue that helps man to avoid enslavement.

We must not let the moralists, the socialists, and the revisionists win. We must call them out on their lies and their misrepresentations of facts. We must go on the offensive at the ballot box and the soapbox. We must take the moral high ground of capitalism, self-reliance, and self-government. Our lives, our liberty, our pursuit of happiness rests in the balance.

Chapter Fourteen

Life, Liberty, and the Pursuit of Happiness

We hold these truths to be self-evident, that all men are created equal, that they are endowed by their creator with certain unalienable Rights, that among these are Life, Liberty, and the Pursuit of Happiness--

We all have hopefully read these words many times. But do we truly understand them?

When Thomas Jefferson wrote that we are all created equal, what did he mean? Some statists would like you to believe that he meant we should try to equalize people monetarily. But Jefferson was a man of means. He was an innovator that was familiar with Adam Smith's writings and was an avid capitalist. This definition is ludicrous when you have knowledge of the man it came from. So what did he mean when he said we were all created equal?

Equality means equal opportunity, not equal results. Jefferson had looked at the system of nobility from England and the rest of Europe, and knew that if there was to be liberty in the new country, that equal opportunity must be guaranteed. He also knew that capitalism and Adam Smith's free market were the only means to achieve this.

Men like Bill Gates are living proof that the free market works. He started with only ideas and a willingness to achieve, and built the greatest fortune ever amassed by an individual. His innovations have increased the productivity of the entire world, but yet that was not and is not his intention. His intention was and is to make a profit.

The success of Microsoft would not have been possible under the system of nobility that we threw out with our revolution and subsequent Constitution. In fact, one has to wonder if many of the modern innovations would have came about at all if not for these visionaries like Jefferson and Madison having set up this system of individualistic equality in the first place.

The equal spoken of in the Declaration of Independence was not speaking of Karl Marx's twisted notion of equal outcome, but rather of the nobler concept of equal opportunity, the opportunity to innovate and excel. This is another crucial point, as many of the revisionists would have you believe that our founding fathers never intended for capitalism to be guaranteed.

In the next part of the sentence, Jefferson goes even further by saying that we had been endowed by our creator with unalienable rights. What is an unalienable right?

An unalienable right is a natural right. As Jefferson put it, a right that is endowed upon us by the creator, or a God-given right. This means that we have rights that can not be given or taken away by any government. These rights are ours when we are born, and no man or group of men has the right to take them away.

He goes on to say that among these are life, liberty and the pursuit of happiness. What he is talking about here is freedom. Freedom to live your life as you see fit. Freedom to keep the fruits of your own labor. Freedom to make your own way. Our founding fathers were not perfect men, and they knew that we would also fall short of perfection. They were attempting to set up a system tolerant of different ideals, religions, and philosophies. That's why they attempted to set up, for the first time in history, a government that recognized the individuals rights, and this notion of liberty. Jefferson himself defined liberty as; *" Of liberty I would say that, in the whole plenitude of its extent, it is unobstructed action according to our will. But rightful liberty is unobstructed action according to our will within limits drawn around us by the equal rights of others. I do not add 'within the limits of the law,' because law is often but the tyrant's will, and is always so when it violates the right of an individual."*

Jefferson had much to say on the subject of rights;

"It is to secure our rights that we resort to government at all."

"The idea is quite unfounded that on entering into society we give up any natural right."

Jefferson was an amazing man and an eloquent speaker and writer. My studies of his writings have forever endeared him to me. The Declaration of Independence, which I parody in this book, is one of the greatest documents ever written. It is fitting that my final Jefferson quote on rights comes from this precious document;

"To secure these Rights, Governments are instituted among Men, deriving their just powers from the consent of the Governed That whenever any Form of Government becomes destructive of these Ends, it is the Right of the People to alter or abolish it, and to institute new Government, laying its Foundation on such Principles, and organizing its Powers in such Form, as to them shall seem most likely to effect their Safety and Happiness."

The Constitution goes on in detail to define even more of these natural rights. From freedom of the press, to the right to bear arms, these visionaries knew and respected our natural rights. They knew and tried to in some way guarantee that our government should provide protection for these rights. We should demand no less from our constitutionally challenged leaders today.

Chapter Fifteen

The Right to Bear Arms

From the Brady Law to the assault weapons ban to hundreds of other gun laws, our Second Amendment right to bear arms has been under attack. Under the guise of 'for the common good', slowly but surely the political elite are trying to disarm the American people. Arguing that either the Second Amendment is obsolete or that its meaning is somehow unclear, they are trying to convince us that we would somehow be better off without guns. Like getting rid of guns would magically make violence disappear.

Intelligent people can not possibly misconstrue the meaning of the Second Amendment. It reads *"A well regulated militia being necessary to the security of a free state, the right of the people to keep and bear arms, shall not be infringed."* Whose right to keep and bear arms? The people. Not only to keep arms, but to carry them also. Arguments have been made that the first line explains whose right it is, but the first line is referring to the state's right of keeping a militia not associated with the federal military. The second part refers to a natural right of an individual. That is the right to be secure in your being, your personal effects, and your liberty.

The right to bear arms isn't just about hunting, or home protection, or sporting, although these are all good uses for firearms. The reason we must never let ourselves be disarmed is that the right to bear arms was put in place so that, as a last resort, the people have the power in their hands to overthrow tyrants. Many people will cringe at that last statement. They will say that I am anti-government, or a terrorist. You will not find a more loyal 'citizen' than myself. I love the ideals of our Founding Fathers, and this is one of them. A bumper sticker that I've seen sums it up nicely. *"An armed man is a citizen, an unarmed man is a subject".* Ask the people who elected Adolf Hitler (yes elected, he got almost 90% of the vote), what his first act as chancellor was. You would find that he disarmed the public.

But what good are guns against a modern military? Here's the part that the politicians don't want you to realize. To rid yourselves of tyrants, you don't have to fight the military; you just have to rid yourselves of the politicians themselves. The break-up of the Soviet Union is a good example. There was very little bloodshed since the troops were hesitant to fire upon their own people. If armed conflict between the government and a massive amount of citizens occurred, the armed forces would not be a factor, since they are our brothers and sisters, and since the conflict would mainly be comprised of assassinations and surprise attacks. There are only 537 elected officials at the federal level, and a few hundred top-level bureaucrats. There are over 75 million armed citizens, so you do the math. The only choice the statists would have would be to ask for UN troops to come in. This in turn would anger the rest of the citizenry, and possibly bring the military in on the side of the people. The statists know all of this, and that is why they will lie and cheat and do anything to disarm us. In short, a benevolent government needs armed citizens, while a malevolent one can not tolerate them.

What about assault rifles? First define assault rifle. I have never heard a good definition. Most people's definitions have something to do with the way the gun looks. Is this what we object to? If you say high powered, a double-barreled shotgun is a very powerful gun. If you say high capacity magazines, most .22 long rifles hold 18 rounds. Would you consider either one of these to be assault weapons? But getting past the lack of clear descriptives, this ban is completely unconstitutional. *"Shall not be infringed."* This is what it says. If the Supreme Court tries to say otherwise, they are wrong. Read it yourself. Don't let the statists, like the pigs in the novel "*Animal Farm*" change the words. It makes no exceptions.

How do they want the Second Amendment to read? Maybe something like this:
"*A state run militia, being necessary to the security of the leaders, the right of the people to allow law enforcement to carry weapons shall not be infringed*". If our founding fathers had meant it that way, they would have said it that way. This is not a document of hidden meanings.

But don't just take my word for it. Don't just take Charlton Heston's word for it. Jefferson wrote on many occasions about the right to bear arms. *"One loves to possess arms, though they hope never to have occasion for them."* He felt that is was not just our right, but our duty to be armed; "*None but an armed nation can dispense with a standing army. To keep ours armed and disciplined is therefore at all times important."* Patrick Henry concurred by saying, *"The great object is, that every man be armed"*

So if a man (or woman) is truly anti-gun, they need to do several things. First, they need to put their money where their mouth is. They should put a bumper sticker on their car and a sign in their yard that simply says, "*This is a gun free zone*." Secondly, they should stop voting. That's right, if they can't do their duty by being armed, then they shouldn't vote either. Our republic can not survive if these two duties of citizens are not performed, and one is no more important than the other. Third, they need to sign petitions to amend the Constitution. The only way to legally take our weapons is to amend the Constitution. Until then, they should shut the hell up.

Maybe you think that we should give up our guns. Maybe you think that you should take them away from the rest of us. Just remember when you try this, ***our side is armed you morons***. Just go ahead and put up your sign to let others know how you feel. While your sign tells criminals that you are prepared to be a victim, mine says, "*This home protected by an I'll cap your ass security system.*"

I have taught my son marksmanship and gun safety, and encouraged him to learn ballistics and the science of guns, because I have realized that he is America's future. I realized that as long as we keep making marksmen, our country shall not fall into the hands of would be tyrants. This realization scared me. As I said earlier, millions of America's children are being raised to fear and loathe firearms. Will we be able to defend our country and our freedom if this trend continues?

There is some historical basis for my fear. During the American civil war, the North by all accounts should have made quick work of ending the rebellion. Outnumbered and outgunned, only one thing kept the rebels going as long as they did.

Marksmen.

The southern boys had grown up target shooting, and hunting with their rifles. Many northerners, on the other hand, had bought into the notion that guns were somehow not acceptable in a civilized society. It was difficult for the North to train marksmen and snipers. Science tells us that in order for someone to become truly proficient at something, it is important to start when a person is in his or her formative years. Ask the Swiss people how they were able to stay neutral while surrounded by the Nazis and they will tell you that Hitler knew what the cost would be of trying to overcome a country in which 11 year olds could outshoot his best marksmen.

Dangerous, some would say, teaching a minor how to shoot. But, according to studies, some done by the government, children who are taught how to handle weapons are far less likely to be involved in any crime. In one study while a great number of 'gun-free' children had been involved in gun violence, in the two years in which the study was conducted, not one child who had been taught about guns and gun safety was involved in any crime that involved guns. This report has quietly been shuffled to the side by the media and the bureaucrats.

A recent article about Great Britain touted the banning of all guns there for its lower murder rate than the US. What the obviously anti-gun article failed to mention is that the rape and violent assault rate has since increased, and that bombings, knifings, and poisonings occur at a much higher percentage than here in the USA. Also absent is the fact that if we wanted to be like the British, we wouldn't have kicked them out of our country in 1776. The British don't have freedom of the press either, and quite routinely bar publication of articles that expose wrongdoing within their own government. They still have kings and queens for crying out loud. I would not be able to publish this book there, and I do not wish to emulate their society. No liberty lover should, since their government and laws are basically unchanged since our revolution and separation from them.

Recent events have the anti-gun activists up in 'not arms'. From Columbine to other acts of violence, they point fingers at guns, TV, the NRA, video games, gun manufacturers, anyone but the criminals themselves. This is unacceptable. The blame lies solely with the perpetrators. The bleeding hearts establishment thinks that we should coddle these criminals, find out what could have caused them to be violent and take away their pain. They could not be more wrong. This is all a part of people not wanting to take responsibility for their own lives. "It's not my fault." That's become the battle cry of the criminals and the liberal statists who try to protect them from swift and sure justice. I don't want to feel their pain. They have inflicted enough already. Put them away for good, or put them to death for they have no place in a free society. But maybe that's the point. These statists do not want to live in a free society, so in their utopian world maybe they think there is room for monsters.

Knowing that they haven't been able to get their laws in effect, (the Constitution gets in their way), the anti-gun movement recently has focused on lawsuits. Since the burden of proof is lower in a civil trial, they have now started suing gun makers. They seek monetary damages, but not for any victims. They seek money so they can sue more and eventually put the gun makers out of business. The courts should also look at this as unconstitutional. If the plaintiffs get what they seek, it would effectively cancel the Second Amendment. They also have not realized that if they ever succeed at this ploy, many like myself will sue the anti-gun groups. In fact, some already have, and others are now planning to.

Statists and anti-gun activists need to understand clearly that for many this issue is their personal point of critical mass. There are many people, including myself that consider the right to bear arms as the cornerstone of America. Without it, we become a nation enslaved. The more they push to control and ban weapons, the more weapons we will collect, for in our hearts and minds we know that we are yet another step closer to having to rely on them to restore our freedom. Good government has nothing to fear from an armed citizenry. Bad government does. Perhaps this is why many of them would like us to do as the Socialist Diane Feinstein says and "*Turn them in, turn them all in.*" Instead of turning them in, as long as there are statists running our 'free' nation like Ms. Feinstein and Mr. Schumer, who has a passion to legislate (force), we need to collect more.

We have the natural right to protect ourselves. I have the natural right to protect my life, liberty, and my pursuit of happiness. Don't just give lip service to these words, they have meaning. This is the issue that we must by all means stand firm upon.

I will not be disarmed. Yes, there will be abuses. There will be murders and violence. That is the price we must pay for liberty. It's too late to arm yourself when concentration camps, rape camps, mass graves, and bloody streets surround you. It is too late to say, "I didn't know this would happen," or "I wish I had kept my guns." How many times do we need to see that absolute power corrupts absolutely? How many times must we be dragged out of our homes and herded like cattle into some slave, rape or death camp? I, and others of like mind, will not go quietly or peacefully. They will take my ammunition one bullet at a time, and they will have to pry my guns from my cold dead fingers if they want them. They better bring help, because I won't be alone.

Chapter Sixteen

The Military

The most basic and most important function of any nation's government has historically been its military. No matter what form that government has taken, no country has ever stood for long without a strong military. Our forefathers knew this, and tried to provide for it. They also enacted rules to try to ensure its wise use.

There is no doubt that we in America are blessed with having the finest and the most powerful military in the world. Our military has shown again and again that it has no equal. Our civilian leadership of it however, has in modern history been suspect. What did our founding fathers say about the military and its use, and how would this apply to our modern military with its unparalleled weaponry?

You hear the experts and politicians talk about the challenges our military faces today, and they make this a crisis, and that a crisis, and before you know it, they are asking for more money from the taxpayer. What the military needs however, is better leadership and fewer tasks assigned to it by our modern masters. From digging wells in Haiti, to policing the streets of Sarajevo our military is performing functions that they are not only unequipped to do, but are also unconstitutional and unwise.

Our founding fathers led a bloody revolution against tyrants, and knew the importance of the military. But they also knew the importance of using it properly. Jefferson warned us about staying out of the affairs of other nations; *" Commerce with all nations, alliance with none, should be our motto."* He went on to say; *"To take part in conflicts would be to divert our energies from creation to destruction."*

Not only are these modern intrusions into the sovereign affairs of other nations unconstitutional, they can be counter-productive. By interfering we sometimes make things worse, but more importantly, we create enemies. By militarily and monetarily supporting dictators such as the Shah of Iran, we created the catalyst for the Infahda or holy war against the United States by many Moslems. Think of all of the bloody incidents in modern history, and how they could have been avoided completely if we had heeded our forefathers advice and stayed out of the affairs of other nations. The hatred of the United States, by people in other nations is a direct result of our interference. We should lead by example, not by force or monetary coercion.

What's even worse, is our leaders insistence of United Nations interference in the affairs of other sovereign nations. By interfering in other nations' affairs, they are setting us up for the other nations naturally assuming that they can interfere in ours. There is already a call to do so in the case of our Second Amendment. The United Nations already calls for all nations to disarm their citizenry, and point fingers at the United States for not doing so. We should not only quit this socialistic organization that purports to be the world's government, but we should kick them completely out of this country. A bill pending in Congress sponsored by congressman Ron Paul of Texas would do just that.

In order for our country to remain free, we must heed the advice of our forefathers. Not only to stay out of the affairs of foreign nations, but to raise and train our children to desire liberty. This includes training them to handle, use, and bear arms. A free nation will remain so if the populace is trained in protecting itself. Jefferson said much on the subject; *"None but an armed nation can dispense with a standing army. To keep ours armed and disciplined is therefore at all times important, but especially so at a moment when rights the most essential to our welfare have been violated."* Our military is supposed to be able to draw from a pool of trained marksmen. In the event that war does break out, we can protect ourselves while an army is being formed. Jefferson again; "*Uncertain as we must ever be of the particular point in our circumference where an enemy may choose to invade us, the only force which can be ready at every point and competent to oppose them, is the body of neighboring citizens as formed into a militia. On these, collected from the parts most convenient, in numbers proportioned to the invading foe, it is best to rely, not only to meet the first attack, but if it threatens to be permanent, to maintain the defence until regulars may be engaged to relieve them.*"

These quotes not only support the ideals of militias and weapons training by all citizens, but also support a vigorous and strong Second Amendment. One final Jefferson quote on the subject only needs the deleting of the word males to bring it up to modern principles of liberty; *"We must train and classify the whole of our male citizens, and make military instruction a regular part of collegiate education. We can never be safe till this is done."*

This is why responsible gun owners, instead of being vilified by the media, should be thanked and revered. Our colleges, instead of teaching the principles of Karl Marx, and trying to rewrite the Second Amendment, would be much more helpful to the cause of liberty to teach Jefferson and marksmanship. We should take solace in the fact that no foreign power would ever try to invade a nation where there are over 75 million armed citizens.

According to free market principles, in order for any business, industry, or governmental entity to be able to hire enough workers in any given skill, it must pay the going rate, and keep raising the rate of pay and benefit levels until it reaches saturation. This principle also applies to the military. I oppose the draft. The draft goes against the principles of liberty. In any given situation, if the citizens were behind the military action being taken, such as defense of the nation, there would be no shortage of volunteers.

With our modern leaders misusing the military to perform police actions today, it is not easy to maintain the type of public support that is necessary to produce an all volunteer army. The statists know this, and have pushed in greater benefits and pay in an attempt to keep our peacetime armies large. In reality, if we followed our forefathers advice, and kept them at home, downsized in times of peace, and did not use them in unconstitutional ways, we wouldn't have the problems that we now face in recruiting enough soldiers. The fact is, we wouldn't need as many. Jefferson saw the need for small amounts of troops to be kept in times of peace but many times warned of quartering large numbers of troops without a war going on. *"If no check can be found to keep the number of standing troops within safe bounds while they are tolerated as far as necessary, abandon them altogether, discipline well the militia and guard the magazines with them. More than magazine guards will be useless if few and dangerous if many."*

Here again Jefferson not only calls for the army to be smaller in peacetime, but he again mentions the community-based militia. The militia he speaks of is every able-bodied American. He viewed armed citizens as the first line of protection for a free people. This still applies today, regardless of what the anti-gun statists try to tell you.

The military question that seems to be plaguing all politicians today is how to deal with gays in the military. From kicking out all gays, to don't ask don't tell, no solution will ever satisfy all parties involved. I think the whole subject is overrated, and we need to apply the principles of liberty to it, and move on. The fact is that we have had many gays and lesbians honorably serve in the military. The army of Israel, which allows gays to openly serve, has already answered the question of unit coherence. Here again, I think all people should keep their sexuality private, but should not be compelled to do so.

We need to follow our forefather's wisdom and stop trying to police the world. By doing so, we would not only save billions of dollars of taxpayers' money, but would also show leadership by staying out of the affairs of sovereign nations. By concentrating our military efforts into defense instead of offense, our security would be strengthened. We need to stop being the big bully, and start being the defenders of liberty. Other nations, as well as ourselves, should be free to determine their own futures. We should be free to choose our destiny and others must be allowed to do the same.

Our military is our future. But that future must be guarded not only with a federal military, but also the community based militia. Our founding fathers recognized this and even spoke of it in the Second Amendment, which should serve to underscore the importance of it. The military must have a deep well of trained marksmen to draw its soldiers from. We must raise and train our children to not only bear arms, but to treasure them as our insurance against tyranny and oppression from internal and external would be tyrants. The only way for our liberty to be protected is for us to provide ourselves with potential soldiers. Our lives, our liberty, and our future depends on it.

Chapter Seventeen

Race Relations

Let's get one thing straight. Scientifically speaking, there is one race, the human race. We come in all shapes, sizes, colors, creeds, religions, ethnicity, language, sex, and orientation. Let's face it, we are a world of *individuals* as varying and different as we could possibly be.

Some revisionists want you to believe that since many of our founding fathers kept slaves that in some way that makes them or their philosophies somehow irrelevant. What they don't acknowledge is that from the very beginning that many of them tried to free the slaves.

Thomas Jefferson was a slave owner. As modern DNA tests have proven, he most likely even fathered children by one of his slaves by the name of Sally Hemmings. The modern media have made much of this, but most of the time, they don't tell the whole story.

Thomas Jefferson was a philosopher, a self-taught lawyer, a farmer, a politician, an entrepreneur, and an inventor, along with many other talents. He wrote the Declaration of Independence, became our third President, and his writings, speeches, and influence on the founding of this nation is generally acknowledged to be of paramount importance. He also owned slaves.

When he wrote the Declaration of Independence, he along with some of the other delegates wanted to free the slaves. Many of the arguments by the representatives in Philadelphia were about the issue of slavery. In the end, in order to come to a consensus the phrases that would have freed them were dropped from the document. But what was left, I believe Jefferson knew would one day be used to help those who were enslaved. Read the Declaration. *"All men are created equal."* There can be no doubt what he had in mind for the future. He often spoke on the subject and one of my favorite quotes is; *"Nobody wishes more ardently to see an abolition, not only of the trade, but of the condition of slavery; and certainly, nobody will be more willing to encounter every sacrifice for that object."*

As for Sally Hemmings, his so-called affair with her most likely came after his wife had died. She was his dead wife's half-sister and by all accounts she looked very much like her. She stayed with him for the rest of his life, even when he was in France *where she was free.* She could have left but didn't. He also freed every one of her relatives. To me that speaks volumes about their relationship.

From the very start there was trouble in the new nation over slavery. There had been many deals between the slave and free states over the course of the new nation's journey. There had been many arguments in Congress, and rightly so since it was imperative that a nation built on liberty should apply that liberty to all. The Civil War was an inevitable occurrence. The revisionists now want you to believe that the Civil War was not about slavery, but about state's rights. This half-truth is a slap in the face to all that fought to abolish slavery.

Yes, the Union fought to preserve the nation, and felt that states did not have the right to secede. But make no mistake, from the outset it was about slavery. Abraham Lincoln, knowing that the root cause of the war was slavery, and wanting to insure that it would not be fought in vain, wrote the Emancipation Proclamation that effectively ended slavery in the United States.

Eventually, even though the southern soldiers fought hard and honorably, the North and the ideals of liberty for all won the day. It was not a dark day for the south as some would have you believe, but it was a bright day for America. Many had fought and died on both sides, and it was time to put the nation together again and to heal the wounds.

The ideals put forward by our forefathers now applied to all. Black, white, Asian, no matter what a person's heritage, they were now legally equal. It took several generations, and many heroes and martyrs like Rosa Parks and Dr. Martin Luther King to accomplish the promises of our forefathers to all. There is still work to be done, in the hearts of men, and in changing some of the laws that act more to incite racism than to abolish it.

The laws that I refer to are the ones that force inequality on people, businesses, and government agencies. We call these laws 'affirmative action', but what they are in reality are racist attempts at equal outcome. Anytime the law holds one group's rights above another's it is racist.

Some would have you believe that the white people in this country in some way owe the blacks for slavery. There is not one person living today that either was a slave, or a slave owner. Most of our ancestors never owned slaves in the first place. Also, the Constitution strictly prohibits punishing descendants for their ancestor's crimes even if the crime was treason. Last but not least, using this reasoning, wouldn't Christians owe Moslems and Pagans for the crusades? Would Italians owe Jews for Rome's enslavement of them? Would Africans owe their American descendants for selling them into slavery in the first place? It is easy to see that the politics of paying back descendants of injustice could take up all of our time. We should instead be getting about the business of living today.

Equality is equal opportunity, not equal outcome. The question of race should never be asked, much less used as a prerequisite for any job or benefit. Businessman Ward Connerly has led the charge against preferential treatment, and he uttered one of my favorite quotes when he said; "*Rosa Parks didn't refuse to sit in the back of the bus so that only black people could sit in the front, she did it so that all people could sit in the front.*"

Racism still exists, but all races are guilty of it. Typical American mutts like myself don't understand the arguments and strife, since most of us were descended from a variety of different immigrant and native cultures. We are all Americans plain and simple. Not African-Americans, nor Irish-Americans, not any one of hundreds of ethnic groups prefixing American, but just plain American. We are all descended from people who were expelled or unwanted in their countries of origin. The slaves that came to this country were sold into slavery by their own people. Some of my ancestors were indentured servants, a form of slavery that was quite common. Many came over to escape from religious intolerance, and most faced hardships. We must get over this categorizing of ourselves before we can ever get past it.

This categorizing of people includes profiling by the police. They should not be able to use skin color as the sole purpose for stopping passengers in airports or cars on the freeway. Driving while black is not a crime. This is yet another example of government telling us to do as they say and not as they do. It is wrong for cab drivers to drive past someone simply because they are black or Hispanic. It is equally wrong for cars to be stopped by the police for the very same reasons. In the first case, the government oversteps their authority arresting and even taking away cabs from those suspected of bias. Again, the free market could solve this problem much more efficiently. Boycotts and civil suits would be much more effective in ridding our cities of these types of cabbies than government intrusion into privately owned companies ever could. In the second case, law enforcement claims either that they are not profiling, which is absurd, or that it is a valuable law enforcement tool, which is scary.

The only way to ever rid ourselves of racism is not to allow these divisions and this categorizing in the first place. Having a Miss Black America contest is just as offensive to me as if someone held a Miss White America. I wouldn't watch either. I do not like any groups or organizations that try to divide us as a people. To me, as well as many others, this question of racial division is in itself offensive. I do not answer questions of race on any forms, especially on any type of government forms.

This type of thing only breeds more hatred and division. I have no doubt that the resurgence of hate groups in our modern era has been fueled by affirmative action and preferential treatment of one group over another. It is now the EEOC and affirmative action that furthers racism. Some people hate simply for the love of hating. No amount of legislation will ever change that. It is high time that we get rid of such laws and all just get along as Rodney King put it.

Chapter Eighteen

Jack-booted Thugs and Tyrants

Our forefathers called the king and his henchmen tyrants. The Declaration of Independence recites the transgressions committed against the colonists. It refers to him (King George) as the tyrant many times.

One of the major complaints was that his troops and officers murdered innocent citizens, and then were protected by mock trial from prosecution. The following two stories have yet to be told correctly by the mainstream press. They are disturbing, sad, and more important than you can imagine.

On a hot August day in 1992, federal officers prepared to serve a warrant on a wanted man. This was no ordinary criminal, but one who had cut off a shotgun barrel a half an inch too short. They had tried for months to get the amateur gunsmith to do something, anything illegal so they could arrest him. You see, he was a white separatist, believing that whites and blacks should live separately. Never mind that some black groups like the Nation of Islam preach the same garbage. Never mind that this man never once had preached violence. Never mind that he had only attended a few picnics by the hate group that the government had been investigating. They needed a stool pigeon, and they had threatened to take this man's home and family away from him if he didn't cooperate. He and his family had in effect told the government to shove it. This called for drastic action by the government, and by golly they would go after the dastardly culprit and his family.

As the federal marshals approached the home of Randy Weaver, the Weaver's dog Striker must have heard them coming. The dog went off in the direction of the marshals, barking as he ran. The Weavers naturally thought he had caught the scent of game. Randy's young son Sam and a family friend, Kevin Harris, took their rifles and followed the dog. As the dog neared them, the marshals shot and killed it. The marshals still had not identified themselves, and Sam must have surely thought that they were out to harm him and his family so he opened fire. So did Kevin Harris, and the marshals. When the smoke had cleared, Sam, a marshal named Degan, and the dog Striker all lay dead. Sam had been shot in the back, presumably as he had tried to flee.

The marshals that remained sent a message down to the sheriff that they had been in a horrendous firefight, and that over a thousand rounds had been fired at them, much of it from the back of a pickup truck. The truth was 14 shots had been fired by the marshals, 5 shots by Sam and Kevin, and there was no pickup truck.

In response to the lies told by the marshals about the extent of the gun battle, the FBI dispatched its elite snipers known as the Hostage Rescue Team. The men in charge then illegally changed the rules of engagement from 'officers can open fire when threatened', to 'shoot all armed adults'. This was to promote an unwritten rule among federal agents, that if one of their own was killed the perpetrators should not be taken alive.

After a horrible night for the Weavers (they had lost their son), dawn came to Ruby Ridge. There still had been no warnings, or communication from the federal authorities. Randy, his daughter Sara, and Kevin walked out of the house to go say goodbye to Sam, who they had laid in the shed the night before. As Randy reached to open the shed, an FBI sniper by the name of Lon Horiuchi opened fire and hit Randy in the underarm.

The three of them then took off for the house running and yelling. Randy's wife Vicki, still inside the house, heard the commotion and had opened the door, and held it open. The sniper Lon Horiuchi squeezed off another round. This one blew half of Vicki's head off and lodged in Kevin's chest.

Over the next few days, the FBI would taunt the remaining Weavers about their dead mother and wife Vicki, whose body rotted in front of her children and husband before the standoff was over. The government had said that they would take his home and family away if he didn't cooperate, and they had effectively done just that.

In the aftermath of Ruby Ridge, as it has come to be known, several things have happened. Randy Weaver was found not guilty of all charges except failure to appear on the charge of the sawed-off shotgun. Kevin Harris was found to have acted in self-defense in the death of Marshal Degan. Randy won a multi-million dollar wrongful death lawsuit against the government. Of course, none of this could bring Mr. Weaver's family back.

But what of the real criminals in this case, the overzealous, we are the supreme power, jack-booted thugs who killed innocent women and children?

One agent was suspended and two others reprimanded over a whitewash investigation into the murderous incident. The US Attorney's Office was found to have engaged in misconduct. The on scene commander Eugene F. Glenn was suspended for 15 days and the assistant director in charge, Larry Potts, was promoted to Deputy Director of the FBI. A mother and a son, neither of whom were ever charged with a crime, were dead and no one was ever prosecuted in their deaths. The ATF was criticized for the act that had started the whole mess, the entrapment of Randy Weaver, and trying to bully him into setting others up.

Let's move a year forward now. The government surely learned some lessons, right? It was February 1993. The new Clinton Administration was just starting to spread its wings. The ATF had grown concerned about a group of religious zealots in Waco Texas who seemed to be collecting guns. Never mind that there were several licensed gun dealers among this group known as the Branch Davidians, and that their leader, David Koresh, had invited the ATF to inspect their weapons, at the Mt. Carmel center as they called it. The ATF had gotten a black eye over their handling of Ruby Ridge, and with Senate appropriation hearings just a week away, they needed the publicity that a large raid, with the press watching, would provide.

From the outset, it was doomed to fail. The press had jumped the gun, so to speak, and arrived a half-hour before the ATF agents. One of the members of the media actually called inside the center and tipped off the families as to what was coming. The agent in charge, knowing they had lost the element of surprise, still went forward with their plan of attack.

They had been planning and training for an all-out assault on the center for months. The ATF had lied to the military and said they were training for a drug bust in order to use the military's equipment and their facilities to train. They were prohibited by law to use them for any other purpose.

All that was left was to get a warrant. It was quite an interesting one too; two-thirds of the warrant was about the alleged abuse of children, *which is not under the ATF's jurisdiction.*

Local law enforcement, which did have jurisdiction, had investigated the child abuse charges before, but could not find enough evidence to press charges.

David Koresh, as government officials knew, often traveled to town alone. They could have easily made an arrest there, and then served the search warrant at the Mt. Carmel Center.

But the ATF needed a big show, and they got one.

The ATF pulled up to the center with over 30 agents in cattle trailers. What happened next is a matter of contention. The ATF claims that the Branch Davidians fired first and ambushed them. The evidence, and everyone who wasn't a federal officer on the scene that day, say it was the ATF who fired first.

First, examine the way that the ATF arrived. If the Branch Davidians were bent on ambushing them, reason dictates that they would have started the fight while the agents were still close together in the cattle trailers, while they were easy targets.

Secondly, much of the evidence pointing to who fired first has mysteriously disappeared. The door, which the ATF claims the

Branch Davidians had shot through to begin the battle, is missing. How can you lose a metal door? Reporters and local law enforcement that saw the door say that almost all of the holes were indented on the outside, and had metal shards protruding from the inside. This would tend to indicate that at least the majority of the rounds fired in the initial battle had been fired into the complex, and not from it.

Then there is the mysterious blank tape. The ATF had professionally videotaped the raid, and the first tape, which would have shown the beginning of the firefight, is blank. Mighty convenient, wouldn't you say?

The biggest inescapable fact about the initial gun battle, consistent with the Branch Davidians just defending themselves, came at the end of the attempted raid.

After the gun battle in which several agents and one Branch Davidian were killed, and many on both sides wounded; After helicopters, with armed agents inside had opened fire on a group of buildings that were known to house many women and children (remember the search warrant); After the ATF was out of ammunition; They asked for a cease-fire, and the Branch Davidians agreed. They could have killed every agent. They had them pinned down and out of ammo. Why would a group, hell-bent on ambushing the ATF agree on a cease-fire? They would not have. This leaves no doubt that the Branch

Davidians were defending themselves, and were not the aggressors.

This point is crucial to understand just how important Waco is. Under the rule of law, even if law enforcement has a properly obtained warrant, if they begin by using excessive force, the suspects are within their rights to defend themselves. Juries agreed, and all 11 survivors were found to have acted in self-defense in the deaths of the slain ATF agents.

The ATF did not have ambulances standing by, and members of the press had to call 911 for them. They had phones at their press center, but no communications at the actual scene. This shows that the major concern of the ATF was the publicity of the raid, and not the children. Remember that the search warrant was mainly based on protecting the children within the center.

They claim that there were no reports written by the agents who were at the scene, but this is standard procedure for any incident in which shots are fired. Internal memos that have surfaced show that when they started their mandatory shooting review, the US Attorneys Office told them to stop, because they would create evidence that would find the Branch Davidians innocent.

After the cease-fire, the ATF took a backseat, and let their jack-booted cousins, the FBI take over. The FBI's first move was to move the press 2 miles away. So much for freedom of the press.

The FBI then proceeded to militarize the conflict. They brought in armored vehicles including tanks, and began at daily news conferences to put a military spin on all the events. 'Mt Carmel Center', as the Branch Davidians called it, was changed to 'Branch Davidian Compound' by the FBI. The inventory of weapons by licensed gun dealers within the center became a 'stockpile'. They also referred to Koresh as a cult leader in order to bring up images of Jonestown in the mind of the public. They said he called himself Jesus Christ, but his claim was that he was the seventh seal, or final messiah before the Second Coming of Christ. This was beside the point anyway.

Their religious beliefs had no place in these press conferences. We do still have freedom of religion. These references were only made in an attempt to garner public support for the massacre already being planned by the FBI.

Remember the unwritten rule about not taking suspects alive who had killed a federal agent? The FBI now appointed themselves judge, jury, and executioner.

They claimed that Koresh had duped the people inside, but they included Harvard graduates and people from all walks of life. They were there because they wanted to be there.

They said Koresh and his followers were crazy, yet they used psychological warfare tactics against them.

They would not allow family members to talk to the people inside, which any negotiator will tell you is standard procedure in bringing any situation to a peaceful closure.

According to witnesses, one agent told Koresh's grandmother's attorney that he hoped she had said goodbye. They knew he was to be executed, along with the innocent women and children inside.

They asked Koresh's followers to come out, but those who did were paraded in handcuffs and jail garb in front of cameras so that the Branch Davidians knew what was in store for any others who surrendered.

On April 19, 1993 the FBI moved to complete their planned execution of those who would dare oppose and kill government agents. Using military CS gas and military equipment, they shot poison into the compound. They knew full well that there was not a gas mask made that would fit a child, and that the military CS gas would kill them. Thermal imagery filming from a spy plane above the center seems to show the FBI shot anyone who tried to come out. Twenty-seven of the bodies were found with bullet wounds being the cause of death. The FBI's contention that they did not fire one shot is a lie pure and simple. More than one independent analysis of the thermal imagery has determined that they fired many rounds into the building, and at people trying to escape the fire.

What about the fire, didn't the Branch Dividians set it themselves? That is what the FBI has contended all along, but there is no credible evidence that bears this out. All of the evidence shows that the FBI, either accidentally or purposely set the blaze by firing pyrotechnic grenades into the building, something they denied for 6 years, but finally had to admit to in 1999. What else have they lied about?

They kept firefighters away saying they didn't want them shot, and said they had been fired at from the center, but there is no evidence that the Branch Davidians fired a single shot that day.

While the rubble was still smoking, and the bodies of innocent women and children were still smoldering, the FBI rushed into the rubble and ran the ATF flag up the center's flagpole as if it were a military conquest.

Local law enforcement took a film of the rubble and other evidence at the scene. The FBI demanded the film be turned over to them, and when the locals wanted it back, they were given excuse after excuse until the FBI finally told them they had lost it. Again evidence conveniently disappears.

Local law enforcement saw the federal agents moving things around at the scene before taking pictures, this would be considered tampering with evidence by the courts.

No independent analysis was ever done of the bullets, guns, and cartridges from the scene of the massacre. The FBI has retained possession of all evidence, even telling the Congressional committee that whitewashed the affair that they had lost much of it.

Janet Reno said that the unconstitutional use of military equipment was like renting "...a good rent-a-car". She also took full responsibility.

After a close look at all the evidence in this case, one has to conclude that the Branch Davidians did not commit mass suicide, but rather the government committed mass murder. Ms. Reno, the Texas lethal injection needle awaits you.

We as a nation were appalled that Saddam Hussein used chemical weapons and helicopters to attack civilians, while our own government is guilty of the same heinous acts.

The NRA called the government agents at Ruby Ridge and Waco "jack-booted thugs" and this angered many of our tyrant politicians. Former president Bush even resigned his membership. But I say; if the jack-boot fits, wear it.

Chapter Nineteen

Farm Aid Public Style

Thomas Jefferson once wrote; *"Were we directed from Washington when to sow and when to reap, we should soon want bread."* In 1994, recognizing that governmental intervention into farming was destined to have disastrous effects, the Republicans promised to end farm subsidies. Now 6 years later, the subsidies have increased by the billions.

Politicians have long used farm subsidies to keep themselves in power. They know that cheap food keeps the masses happy. Some people don't have a problem with this. They like having cheap food even if the price is artificially low (temporarily). But these people obviously do not see the long-term implications of these types of policies.

Artificially low prices mean that the farmers are now dependent on handouts from the government. By keeping prices low, they can not profit from a crop. They can only grow it, and collect their money from the taxpayer. What's worse, is that sometimes they get paid not to grow. This is in response to the free markets adjustment to government intervention. Before long all of these subsidies are intertwined and it's hard to sort out which ones are causing the immediate problem, so in an attempt to fix the market, more subsidies are placed into effect. This matches the political solution of choice, to throw more money at a problem, *when the correct answer is just the opposite.*

The free market though, has something that the politicians do not like when it comes to food, its called fluctuating prices. In the free market, the laws of supply and demand dictate prices. When there is too much corn grown, the price falls. This will cause some farmers either not to grow corn the next year, or not to grow as much. The price will be determined by the shorter supply the next year, and if the demand either stays the same or is increased, the price will rise. If the government steps in and subsidizes the farmers, they will all grow more the next year in order to receive more subsidy. Then to stop the inevitable over-production of corn, the government has to pay some farmers not to grow it. This is an oversimplification of the problem, but anyone can see that once the government intervenes into the free market, that the cycle of itch and scratch has begun.

Even more destructive for our economy though, is the practice of bailing out failing farms. This may cause even more people to cringe, but it must be said. By bailing out failing farms, we are rewarding failure. There is a reason why these farms are failing. Free market forces are sometimes not pretty, there are winners and there are losers, but society as a whole benefits from the weeding out of bad ideas and practices.

Capitalism does produce winners and losers, and this is apparent especially in agriculture. But the alternative is a centrally planned socialistic approach, which produces nothing but losers. Look at the Soviet Union's failure to capitalize (sic) on having the most fertile agricultural region in the world.

Jefferson knew that central planning does not work, not only with agriculture but also with all domestic matters; *"Our country is too large to have all its affairs directed by a single government. Public servants at such a distance, and from under the eye of their constituents, must, from the circumstance of distance, be unable to administer and overlook all the details necessary for the good government of the citizens; and the same circumstance, by rendering detection impossible to their constituents, will invite public agents to corruption, plunder and waste."*

Our founding fathers were in tune with farming, as a great many of them were farmers themselves. Thomas Jefferson, among other things, was a highly successful farmer. He invented many farming tools and practices that are still used today, including contour plowing. Eight other signers of the

Declaration of Independence were farmers. So in an attempt to get their original intent, we will again look to the Federalist Papers.

In Federalist Seventeen Hamilton writes, *"...the supervision of agriculture and of other concerns of a similar nature, all those things, in short, which are proper to be provided for by local legislation, can never be desirable cares of a general jurisdiction."* He goes on to elaborate on the state government powers and it becomes quite clear in Federalist Seventeen that agriculture is to be regulated by the state governments, not the federal government. This makes the Department of Agriculture unconstitutional. Their policies make them unwise.

The Department of Agriculture admitted a few years back that food prices were actually 12% higher then they would be without government intervention. But as we have already discussed the reason for the intervention is to lower prices. This happens because the intervention into the free market lowers prices in the short term but has the opposite effect in the long term. Remember that by rewarding failure, innovation is suppressed, so with these subsidies comes the fact that innovations and the weeding out of bad ideas and practices have not occurred in the meantime. This is an attack on the foundation of capitalistic principles.

One more set of facts that makes it quite clear that the Federal Department of Agriculture should be dismantled is the growth of the department itself. In 1900 the department had 3,000 employees to handle 5 million farms. Today the agency has over 60,000 employees to handle about 2 million farms. Looks like Jefferson was right when he said, "*...government tends to grow.*" How long farmers will is another story.

Chapter Twenty

Graphs, Statistics, and Other Lies

One of the favorite tools of the politician is the graph. Bar graphs, pie graphs, and graphs of all shapes, styles, sizes and colors for our enjoyment. The problem is that the graphs are not always correct, and the statistics used to make them are deceptive. One example I remember seeing was a graph of the 1980's earnings increases for the top 5 percentile of Americans. It was a line graph and the politician using it said that the rich had taken much in the decade, and should now foot more of the tax bill. I found a copy of this graph, and it was correct. The problem was they left something out. If this rising line graph is compared with the entire national income for the same period, the bumps and rises are the same. Also if you put a graph up of the taxes these same people paid, it would also match the first. But the most insidious thing was not the graph, or what was left out (a comparison), but rather the statement and conclusion from the politician. It shows that he either does not understand economics, or he does and is lying to get support for his socialist agenda. The rich whom the politician said had taken so much, had in reality created the economic boom, created the wealth they owned, and created wealth and jobs for millions of others. The rest of us had benefited from their creation of wealth. So the graph was used to try to evoke a desired response, even though it was misleading.

The press likes to quote statistics from all kinds of sources. One statistic I read in a newspaper stated that by having a gun in your home, you were far more likely to shoot a family member than a criminal. The problem was that the obviously anti-gun statistician had added women who had shot abusive spouses, ex-spouses, boyfriends, and ex-boyfriends, into the equation. With this data on the proper side, a gun in the home was far more likely to be used against a criminal than on an innocent family member. The other statistic in the same article claimed thousands of children were shot in the US during the previous year, but they included in the data adults as old as 21 as children. The truth is that 44 children under the age of 10 had died from the result of gunshot wounds *in the entire US* the previous year. The death of a single child is a tragedy. But don't use it dishonestly to further a political agenda. All statistics should be suspect unless they give a full accounting of the data used to arrive at the numbers.

The other misleading tool used by the press as well as politicians is the poll. Polls are taken with an outcome in mind before the first question is asked. Then by manipulation of the order of questions, what is said between the questions, or simply by the wording of the question, they trap people into giving the answers that the pollsters want. For example, one pollster from an anti-drug group called my home, and quoted statistics about how many children were hooked on drugs and how many had died. Then he asked if I thought that more money should be spent on rehabilitation or on law enforcement. I'm quite sure that they never used my answer in their data! First, they evoked the emotion, using suspect statistics about children and drugs. Next, they asked me to make a choice of where to spend more money, never asking if I thought we should spend less. They had an assumption of how they wanted the results to look before they asked the questions.

Many times, people define things differently. Remember Bill Clinton saying he had never had sex with Monica Lewinsky? Then we found out that he personally did not define oral sex as sex. As I said before, he should have told Ken Starr and everyone that kept asking about his sex life to go to hell. But this example shows how words can be twisted and redefined to mean what we want them to mean.

It is only natural for people to use statistics, graphs, polling data, or to even twist the English language to affirm their cause, and disregard that which goes against their agenda. By knowing this we should always be wary of polls, statistics, graphs, and just about anything else that comes out of a politician's or their henchmen's mouths.

Chapter Twenty-one

Economics

Many people have very little understanding of economics, and as I studied and researched for this book, I discovered that my own knowledge was lacking. Let's face it, the subject of macroeconomics is tedious and boring. Because of this we tend to defer global economic policy and domestic economic policy to our leaders. The problem is they will lie to us about other things, so you know they will lie to us about money. In fact, probably more so. Not only that, many of them have misconceptions or flawed (Marxist) philosophies when it comes to money.

Bill Gates at the last count was worth over 80 billion dollars. I've heard people comment that he should give some of that money back to the people who made it for him, or that no one should have that kind of money, or that he took more than his share. This shows a complete lack of understanding of capitalism.

The money supply is not like a pie being divided up. When one person gets more, it does not take from anyone else's share. Instead, when an entrepreneur comes up with a product or a service, the money supply increases. Not only for the entrepreneur, but also for all suppliers, workers, shippers, and any others that do business with them. These people in turn are able to spend more, creating a ripple effect out into the communities. Bill Gates created wealth by putting out a product that increased productivity, therefore his impact on the economy has been in the trillions of dollars. This means he has only received a fraction of the wealth that he created. How many small businesses have been started as a direct result of the computer boom, which was accelerated by Bill Gate's software? If an inventor builds and markets a product, the only loser will be an inferior competitor. The invention will create jobs, expanding the money supply and create wealth for many including the inventor. If a small business opens to provide a service, there again the money supply increases; there is no 'pie' to be divided differently.

Even the inferior competitor gains in many situations, as in the case of software. Microsoft's inferior competitors have increased their sale because products like Windows increased the overall market. Even those who are now crying foul should be thanking Bill Gates for increasing their sales. Their companies would not be nearly as large as they are today without Microsoft's gigantic impact on the computer industry. The technical aspects of computers put off consumers until Windows simplified them. I can remember the frustration of operating a computer before Microsoft's products. The first time that I used a computer with Windows, I knew that the age of computers had arrived. Thank you Bill Gates.

Recently a commercial has been playing on TV with an HMO bragging about being a not-for-profit enterprise. Most people would look at that favorably, as we know insurers make too much profit. Or do they? How much is too much profit? In a capitalistic economy, there can be too much profit in just one way. Monopoly. A business that holds a monopoly can for a short period of time (until competitors go after their business), make excessive profits. This holds true even for the mixed economy we now have.

Today, there is another type of monopoly. One that can only be created by government intervention into the economy, one that can remain viable for a long time. It's called a coercive monopoly. Insurance is mandatory on vehicles, so even though there are competing companies, they know you have to buy it, so the market pressures to lower rates is never brought into play. Laws that mandate that individuals or businesses purchase specific products, create coercive monopolies that will charge too much.

Another common misconception is the free ride that so appeals to some. A commercial on television offered information on 'free' government money. The problem is that the money came out of our pockets. I was outraged. How many ways can I say that there is no free lunch? Someone always has to pay, and in the case of tax money, someone has to pay at gunpoint. Many people, including myself only pay income taxes because we are forced to. I do not agree with forcefully taking away what one man has earned, and giving it to someone who hasn't. If I desire to give to charity, I will. But I should not be forced to give to charity.

Again, equality means equal opportunity, not equal results. There is no greater injury to man than to let an inferior idea win. This can not happen in pure capitalism. Only through coercion of our government, can inferior products and ideas stay afloat in the marketplace. Government interference or inferior ideas are the primary reasons businesses fail.

Consumers should be the ultimate voice in what products are produced, and which of them are best. Government should not make that decision for us. Many people thought that the Sony Beta format for videotape was better, and that the government should have forced other manufacturers and importers to use that format. The consumers however, liked the longer VHS format better, and its design won in the long run. The same arguments have been made about computers (Apple vs. PC) and we see that the consumers have chosen the PC. For whatever reasons, the consumer in reality votes on the winning design or product. That is really what buying a product is in a free market; voting with money for the products of our choosing.

Since the dawn of man, it has been a dog eat dog world. The free market can not be held back. When government interferes with the free market, the result is the creation of black markets. Illicit drugs would not be the multi-billion dollar industry that it is if drugs were legal. This is the way of the free market. Remember the basics of supply and demand. When the supply of a product is either cut, or impeded, but the demand is the same, the price will rise, profits rise, and the number of individuals supplying it will increase. This is true of all products; there is no difference between legal and illegal when it comes to basic economic rules like supply and demand.

One other point that many people fail to see is that consumption creates wealth. We Americans are constantly being criticized for being a consumer nation. But if we did not consume, we would not produce. Consumption can not occur without production, and production depends on consumption. They are two sides of the same coin. By consuming, we complete the circle of creating wealth that began with production. Everyone that handles a product from producer, to distributor, to retailer, to all of the suppliers of related items like packaging, machinery, and advertisers, make profits. They pay their workers, who in turn consume, and the ripple effect continues to widen as long as the fruits of their labor are not forcefully taken away and wasted by government. This is the way of free enterprise, and one of the reasons that government should be small.

The American Revolution was not as much a revolution against England as it was a revolution in economic thought. Earlier in the century, capitalism and free market forces like greed had been recognized by the economist Adam Smith. The United States was the first country formed on the premise and the promise of capitalism. Jefferson; *"The system of the United States is to use neither prohibitions or premiums. Commerce there regulates itself freely and asks nothing better."*

Our forefathers were quite aware of free-market forces. Jefferson again; *"I think all the world would gain by setting commerce at perfect liberty".* They placed into the Constitution many rules designed to keep the market free of governmental control. But our modern masters have reinterpreted these rules, and in some cases disregarded them completely. Instead of following Adam Smith's advice, they would rather follow Karl Marx. Instead of holding capitalism up as a beacon, they would rather lead us down the dark path of socialism.

In Federalist 41, Madison shows a keen knowledge of enterprise, and makes the argument that the general welfare clause is very limited in its scope. In number 45 he goes on to say, *"The power delegated by the proposed Constitution to the federal government are few and well defined".* This particular quote applies to nearly every chapter of this book. In the Constitution itself Article One section eight gives Congress not the executive branch the power; *"To regulate commerce with foreign nations, and among the several states, and with the Indian tribes".* If they had intended for Congress to be able to regulate all commerce, they would have stopped at the first three words. If they had intended for the various executive branch departments to be able to regulate commerce, they would have said it. A reading of the Constitution and the Federalist Papers makes it quite clear that the federal governments powers over commerce is limited to setting up standard measurements, interstate commerce (highways, DOT, etc.) and making trade agreements with foreign nations. It never gave them the power to go after Microsoft, or the tobacco industry, or the power to make any of the millions of rules the federal government has set on businesses. These kinds of powers are reserved to the states, or prohibited altogether.

As I've said before, many of these regulations are not only unconstitutional, but they are also counterproductive. By over regulating the free market, our modern royalty, in their infinite wisdom, have not only created black markets, they have also created the giant sucking sound that Ross Perot heard years ago. He thought it came from trade agreements, but the rush of industries leaving the United States is caused by over regulation. Many have said that it's because of lower wages in those countries, and in some cases this would be correct. But what is the minimum wage law if not another regulation?

Government tinkering with the free market has caused more problems than it has ever solved. The tinkering with the free market undoubtedly caused the great depression, and more tinkering by the socialist Franklin Roosevelt had made things worse by 1937. It was only because of World War Two (wars are the favorite economic tool of statists), that we were able to come out of the depression.

If there is to be a chicken in every pot, then everyone needs to work, earn money, and buy the chicken. Chicken farmers can not stay in business by giving the chickens away.

Everything costs somebody. When a person is on welfare, the taxpayer pays. When a business or college gets a grant, the taxpayer pays. Every government program, at every level of government is paid for by the taxpayer. Who is the taxpayer?

The primary taxpayers are the working middle class. Most of the taxes are paid by individuals making under $100,000 a year. That includes most of us. Big business and the wealthy are able to reinvest profits, use tax shelters, and hire consultants and attorneys to lower their overall tax burden. The poor of course pay less, because they made less, and in many cases, the funds they receive from the government outweigh the taxes they have paid. So any time they talk about increasing a program, remember it is the middle class who primarily will pay for it.

Capitalism works for all of us, from the working poor, to the middle class, to the very rich. The reason is actually quite simple. Greed.

The rich, in trying to make more money, are encouraged by the capitalist structure into investing in new enterprises. This in turn creates jobs, many of them better paying jobs for the middle class. It also creates jobs to bring some of the poor out of poverty. Keep in mind, that at any point, the lower and middle class can open a business. If they have a good idea, and are willing to work hard, they can become self sufficient or even rich.

The most overlooked fact in economics is that the poor generally rise out of poverty. In other words, the poor of today, were not the poor of years ago. In the early and mid 1980's, I was poor myself. But through hard work, perseverance, and employers who recognized my potential, today I am deeply entrenched in the middle class. This is called picking yourself up by your bootstraps.

My story of rags to middle class is not unusual, or even all that interesting. I still work hard and hope to one day be financially independent, and this is what makes capitalism work so well. The fact that I am willing to try harder, to work harder, to do better, demonstrates what makes capitalism tick. The participants of a capitalistic system are encouraged to always try harder, think better, and innovate.

In comparison, socialists including the ones who call themselves Democrats and Republicans, think that we all should work primarily for the good of society. Under the system that they are quickly putting into place, I would have never picked myself up by my bootstraps, for there would have been no reward for doing so.

Man is guided by his instincts. One of our primary instincts as pointed out by the brilliant 18th century economist Adam Smith, is greed. Capitalism is the only system that is consistent with greed. In fact, capitalism turns greed into an asset. Since individuals are able to pick themselves up out of poverty through hard work and innovation, they are no longer a burden to their neighbors. By creating wealth, money flows out into our communities and makes us all richer.

The least member of any business is actually one of the greatest recipients of its innovations. The floor sweeper has his job, because the people in positions of power have made enough money to pay to have the floor swept. They may not even really need someone to sweep the floor, but they wanted someone to sweep the floor, and were willing to pay someone to do it. That floor sweeper has benefited from all the workers and managers who have turned enough profit to hire him.

Some say that taking care of your fellow man is much more important than profit. I say to them that they are missing the point. By profiting from our endeavors, we have helped our fellow man in a multitude of ways. We have taken care of ourselves first, and not become a burden on our fellow man. We have shared the wealth in our communities by increasing our spending, and therefore the profits of our neighbors. We have in many cases provided jobs and benefits for others. This is the ultimate success of capitalism, that by profiting, the human instinct of greed works to the advantage of all, regardless of their position in the scheme of things.

The progress of mankind in the years since capitalism's conception in comparison to the millions of years of human existence should prove without a doubt, that it is the best and only way for man to proceed into the future.

Capitalism, even the mixed version that we currently have, has created the quality of life that we enjoy today. Think of where we might be if we could once and for all rid ourselves of socialist ideals.

Chapter Twenty-one

Chapter Twenty-two

Free Market Solutions

What good is pointing out the ills of society without also pointing out some solutions? From drugs to welfare there are solutions, albeit some not so popular, that will work. As I will point out, the answers lie in the free-market system and in the freedom we claim to cherish as Americans.

Starting with drugs, we claim to be free, but then we want to tell others what they can and can't ingest into their own bodies. By going after the drugs and dealers, we are not only destroying personal freedom, but we are actually making the problem much worse.

The free market can not be stifled, and whenever governments try, they not only will fail, they also create black markets. When there is a demand, there will be a supply. The more we try to cut this supply, the higher the price gets, creating tremendous cash flows for all involved.

The answer is obviously to decriminalize hard drugs, and legalize lesser drugs like marijuana and ecstasy. By doing so we would cut off organized criminals from their cash supply, be able to regulate purity, and derive some tax benefits. Not only that, but law enforcement could concentrate on crimes where there are actual victims. Billions of dollars now spent on this insane drug war could be given back to the people in the form of lower taxes.

On education, the free market is the only way to get morality back in the schools. Religion has no place in a public school system. But religion can be taught in a private school system.

The teachers unions want you to believe that poor students would not get an education in a private system. There are several holes in this argument.

Under the present system, poor students are getting a substandard education along with middle class students. The only students able to truly get a good education are those whose parents are rich enough to get them into a private school. (Look at where our modern government masters' children go to school.)

A private system would bring the price of private schools down quickly, Remember how the free market works.

Then, these bleeding heart liberals would have a chance to put their money where their mouth is. They could do this by providing scholarships to the private schools of their choice. Of course we know from experience that these types of statists like to force others to pay for their pet issues, but don't ask them to ante up.

Non-profit organizations like churches could step in and create schools that, by the way, could teach religion and morality.

The only solution to our education problems in this country is to privatize the school system. The free market works, and anyone out there trying to convince you otherwise is promoting socialism. It is that simple. Throwing more tax money at the problems only make them worse, and makes we the taxpayers poorer.

One of the major problems we face is the lawsuit shootout going on in the courts. Everyone, it seems, is suing everyone else. Republicans want to limit the amount you can sue for, and the Democrats want the government to join in many of these suits. But there is a free market solution out there. It is called loser pays.

Under loser pays, the loser pays the winner's legal fees. This would not only take the burden off the taxpayer, but it benefits both sides in any dispute. First, the plaintiff's rights are more protected by discouraging frivolous suits. Secondly, the defendants rights are more protected in that the plaintiffs are more likely to settle early, instead of dragging the whole process out. The only real losers under 'loser pays' are the weasel attorneys who under the present system are fleecing us for billions of dollars. This is what makes this good idea hard to implement, because a great many of our leaders are lawyers, weasels, or both.

On welfare, the free market system is much better equipped to deal with poverty than the government ever could be. Welfare only breeds more welfare. Poverty should suck. Individuals should not want to remain impoverished. People should want to work hard and earn their own keep. This may sound cruel, but it is not. In fact it is quite moral, and quite caring to want people to lift themselves out of poverty. It is the American way.

I'm not saying that people shouldn't be able to get help, but what I am saying is that it is not the job of the federal government to give them help. Cities, counties, churches, neighbors, non-profit organizations, and ordinary people are much more efficient, and much more in tune with their own communities' needs.

Many of our problems are tied together, and the free-market solutions for one, are the solutions for the other. For instance we have a higher percentage of our people in jail than any other country including Red China. Our jails and prisons are in a constant state of overcrowding. The statists want you to believe that the answer is to build more and bigger jails. But if we apply the free market solution to illegal drugs, this problem vanishes overnight, since we would then be able to release about 60% of all prisoners, leaving us with more resources to handle the real criminals, the predators of society.

On crime in general, by allowing law-abiding citizens to exercise their constitutionally protected natural right to bear arms, a dramatic drop in crime would occur. Armed citizens don't easily become crime victims, and that's a fact that the anti-gun crowd just can't cope with.

On monopolies, if a company monopolizes a market, and then tries to gouge the consumer, they will not remain a monopoly long. The force of law is the only factor that can enable companies to remain monopolies. By not allowing coercive laws, and by allowing companies to compete in a free-market, we can insure that the consumer will always get the best product at the best price. Individual consumers may not agree with the choices of the majority, but they are always free to use another company's product. In the case of Microsoft, there are other operating systems that will work, they just cost more and don't work as well.

Free-market solutions could solve many of our inherent problems. But there are some problems that no amount of government will ever solve. Many of these, from religious intolerance, to bigotry, to racism, can only be solved in the hearts and minds of the *individual*. These problems can not be solved collectively. The force of law should only be wielded to protect. It is not the panacea for all problems, and when used improperly, it creates more problems than it solves.

Chapter Twenty-two

Chapter Twenty-three

Personal Philosophy

I am, therefore I think. I alone am responsible for myself. I make alliances and acquaintances by my own choice. If I choose to be a friend, I will be. I do not think that the world owes me, or anyone else, a living.

I will make my own path. If I am followed, it is not only because I choose to lead, but also because others choose to follow. If I love, it is by my choice. If I hate, it is by my choice. I do neither easily.

I will not apologize for my achievements, but rather I will bask in them. I am not sorry I deem myself successful, I have worked hard to achieve my goals. I will not apologize for wanting to keep the fruits of my labor. It is my nature and therefore my natural right.

I am not responsible for the actions of my ancestors, but I choose to learn from them, from their successes and failures, from their joys and their sorrows, from their deeds and misdeeds.

I am moral not because of any law or binding, but because I choose to be. My morality is my own, and I will not use the force of law to impose that morality on anyone else. I will not conform to your morality, no matter how many laws you obtain to coerce me to follow it. My morality is not yours, and yours is not mine.

My rights end where yours begin, and by the same token, yours end where mine begin. I am free to do as I choose, as long as I don't encroach on others equal rights to do the same.

My association with others is purely voluntary. I will neither force, nor accept force as a prerequisite for associating with another. My dealings with others are private and I do not recognize any public accounting of my private transactions.

My religion is personal to me, as is yours is to you. I will not tell you what you must believe, and you will not tell me what I must believe. If I choose not to believe at all, then that is my right, and no law or punishment can ever change what is in my own mind.

My mind is my own, and my thoughts are my own property. If I choose to speak, I will. If I choose to be silent, that is my right, and my wisdom.

My body is my own, as yours is your own. If I choose to defile it, it is my right, since it belongs to me. What I choose to put in it is my own business, but I and I alone am responsible for the results.

I am responsible for my own behavior, and I will hold you responsible for yours. Drug addiction, bad childhoods, black rage, demonic possession, and hundreds of others are only lame excuses, and will not relieve you or me of responsibility when either of us overstep our rights and encroach on another's rights.

My property is my own, and if I choose to share it I will. I will resist with all of my being, any attempt to relieve me of it. This is true whether the crooks call themselves lawbreakers or lawmakers. This is true whether the proceeds of the theft will be used to buy crack, or to buy food for the hungry. Theft is theft and a thief is a thief whether he's Jesse James, Robin Hood, or Uncle Sam.

I work for money as well as other reasons. I do not apologize for my greed. I do not apologize for seeking reward. I am not envious of those who have more than I do, but I will let their example be an inspiration. I truly am grateful for the free market, and for the ability of all men to rise above any perceived station.

I will not apologize for capitalism's excesses. Though it has but few faults, it has them none the less. But I would rather live with capitalism's excesses than with socialism's failures. I am not afraid to compete for the brass ring, and I understand that through that competition the world has made its biggest gains.

I am not responsible for your failures and shortcomings, nor are you responsible for mine.

Ask for my help, and you are likely to get it, demand it and you will get my wrath.

I will not use the force of law lightly. It should only be used to retaliate for infringing on one's natural rights. In no case should the force of law be used arbitrarily. That is to say; it should not be used when there has been no victim.

I do not recognize the government's power as omnipotent, and I know that there are those within it who would enslave us. I recognize the individual as the true wielder of power.

I recognize that our natural rights are ours to begin with, and that individual rights do not come from the government, but rather the governments power must come from the people.

I reserve the natural right, as did our founders, to revolt against the government if it becomes too destructive of liberty. The form of that revolt is of my own choosing, whether it is tax evasion, speaking out, voting against republicrats, or as a last resort to join with others and take up arms. There comes a time when we decide that enough is enough. We all have a breaking point, and that point is critical mass.

Chapter Twenty-three

Chapter Twenty-four

Revolutionary

As I was studying our founding documents, an interesting idea struck me. What if these men of great vision and courage were alive today? Surely they would be appalled by our leaders. But as I pondered this, a new idea took shape. What if the events and documents that helped shape our nation were put in modern context? The following was written with tongue firmly in cheek.

Headlines from: The Non-Birth of a Nation

EPA nabs a large mob of suspects after illegal dumping of tea into Boston harbor.

Thomas Jefferson arrested under drug kingpin law, acres of marijuana found at Monticello. In a related story, authorities destroyed his latest literary work called "The Declaration of Independence" after it was discovered that it was written on illegal hemp paper.

The cities of Lexington and Concord have filed suit against Colonial Firearms claiming that the manufacturer caused last weeks gun battle, they also accused the National Musket Association of promoting death and violence.

Dolly Madison killed in ATF raid on Sapphire Ridge. Agents were serving warrant for husband James on charges that he built a musket with a barrel 1/2" too short.

Federal authorities today auctioned off the estate known as Monticello. It was seized from drug kingpin Thomas Jefferson. Under the Rico act, the money raised will be split up amongst all the agencies involved.

Betsy Ross indicted for running sweatshop in the front parlor of her home. Women were sewing without pay in a residential neighborhood. The home was found not to have a business permit.

John Paula Jones claims Washington sexually harassed him while visiting ship.

Branch Quakers killed in battle with cobble-booted thugs in their compound near Waco, Pennsylvania.

Kentucky Long Rifle is banned under new assault musket law.

Ben Franklin under investigation for violation of the anti-trust laws. His company, Franklin Stove, is accused of monopolizing the stove market.

Franklin Stove found to be monopoly. Their bundling of Stovepipe 76 with the stove left competitors out in the cold.

Paul Revere detained after highway search turns up thousands of dollars worth of silver. Officials claim it was going to be used to purchase drugs, and that Mr. Revere couldn't prove otherwise. Local authorities confiscated the silver.

Anonymity on the liberty writing circuit known as the libernet banned. King George promptly hangs Thomas Paine for writing banned e-zine called "Common Sense".

Industry blamed for global cooling that caused that winter's Valley Forge crisis.

Court rules that George Washington must continue funding for painting of American Flag with horsehockey on it.

Lawsuits against musket manufacturers cause largest musket maker to stop selling them to private citizens. Colonists are now fighting the British with sticks and stones.

Continental Congress votes themselves pay raises.

American flag decried by descendants of British as symbol of hatred against them. They demand it not be flown over the Capital.

Mother dies escaping slavery on Underground Railroad. Minor child returned to his father and his master in the south.

Chapter Twenty-four

Chapter Twenty-five

Declaring My Independence

With my sincere apologies to Mr. Jefferson, I will now sign my Declaration of Independence from the Republicrats;

When in the course of human events, it becomes necessary for one's self to dissolve the political bonds which have connected one to a political party, and to join others in demanding the equal station to which the laws of nature and of natures God entitle us, a decent respect to the opinions of mankind requires that I should declare the causes which impels me to the separation.

We hold this truth to be self-evident, that both major parties are dismally equal, that they are endowed by special interest money in infringing on our rights, that among them are those who would be our masters and take away our lives, liberties, and our pursuit of happiness- That to secure our votes they have instituted all forms of trickery and deception amongst men, wielding their unjust power over the heads of the governed, that whenever any party becomes destructive of liberty, it is our right to alter or leave it and join a new party, one with a foundation built on principle, and organizing itself on such form as to it shall seem most likely to effect my safety and happiness. Prudence, indeed will dictate that parties long established should not be left for light and transient causes; and accordingly all experiences has shewn that we are more likely to suffer with inferior candidates from a major party, than to vote for a candidate from a party which we are not accustomed. But when a long train of abusive legislators, pursuing the same money and power, design a system to reduce us to slavery, it is our right, our duty, our destiny, to throw off the major parties and to join the new guardians of liberty. Such has been the patient sufferance of we the voters; and such is now the necessity which constrains us to alter the two-party system of government. The history of our modern government masters is a history of repeated injuries and usurpation's of the Constitution all leading us towards the establishment of absolute tyranny over the people. To prove this, let facts be submitted to a candid world.

They have assented to law after law, mostly unnecessary for the public good, but good for them and their cronies.

They have forbidden the states from passing laws of immediate and pressing importance, and have paramilitary type operations enforcing laws which voters have overturned.

They have refused to pass other laws to accommodate parties other than their own, which leaves large numbers of people without representation in the legislature, a right that belongs to us, and formidable to tyrants only.

They have traveled together to places tropical, comfortable, and distant at the expense of the taxpayer or lobbyist's depository, for the sole purpose of graft.

They have reelected representatives repeatedly; who have in turn repeatedly invaded the private lives of the people.

They have refused for a long time to allow third party or independent candidates to be elected, they have proven themselves incapable of comprehending liberty, and the people have been exposed to the dangers of invasions to our natural rights.

They have endeavored to deceive the population of these states, for that purpose of avoiding prosecution, even from accepting campaign funds from foreigners, and raising funds from public lands.

They have obstructed the administration of justice, by assenting to laws that increase the nanny states power.

They want us to be dependent on their will alone, and having such tenure in their offices as they do, they have steadily increased the amounts and payments of their salaries.

They have created a multitude of new offices, and sent hither swarms of bureaucrats to harass the people and eat out their substance.

They have kept abroad, in times of peace and war, huge standing armies, without clear and present danger to citizens of the United States.

They have affected to render the military dependent to, and inferior to the United Nations One World Government.

They have combined with others to subject us to a UN jurisdiction foreign to our Constitution, and unacknowledged by our laws; giving their assent to their acts of pretended legislation.

For quartering large Bodies of armed ATF, DEA, and other jack-booted thugs among us:

For Protecting them from punishment for any murders which they should commit on the inhabitants of these states:

For cutting off our free trade with all parts of the world:

For imposing taxes on us without our consent:

For depriving us, in many cases the benefits of jury nullification:

For trying us for pretended and non-offenses:

For attempting to abolish the free market system, establishing arbitrary governmental bureaucracies, and enlarging their powers, and attempting to set themselves up with absolute rule into these states:

For taking away our freedom, abolishing our most valuable laws, and altering fundamentally the forms of our government:

For suspending the rights of the people and the states and declaring themselves invested with the power to legislate in all cases whatsoever:

They have abdicated government here, by declaring crisis and waging wars against us.

They have plundered our pockets, ravaged our bank accounts, burnt our crops and homes, and destroyed the lives of our people.

They are, at this time transporting large sums of taxpayers monies to foreign countries, to foreign leaders that rule by death, desolation, and tyranny, already begun with Cruelty and Perfidy, scarcely paralleled in the most barbarous ages, and totally unworthy of the heads of civilized nations.

They have constrained our fellow citizens and taken captive our wages and profits, they have brought arms against the free market, and caused our friends and brethren to rely on handouts from them.

They have excited domestic insurrections and terrorism amongst us, and have endeavored to bring on the inhabitants of our darker side, the merciless anarchist, whose known Rule of Warfare, is undistinguished destruction, of all ages, sexes, and conditions.

In every stage of the oppression we have petitioned for redress in the most humble terms: Our repeated petitions have been answered only by repeated injury. Our modern royalty, whose character is thus marked by every act which may define tyranny, are unfit to be the leaders of a free people.

Nor have they been wanting in their attempts to relieve us of our money. We have warned them from time to time of attempts to legislate unwarrantable jurisdiction over us. We have tried to remind them of our constitutional rights. We have appealed to the justices of our Supreme Court, and we have conjured them by the ties of our common kindred to disavow these usurpations, which, would inevitably interrupt our lives and liberty. They too have been deaf and dumb, to the voice of justice, and of their constituents that are not campaign contributors. We must therefore acquiesce in the necessity, which denounces our separation, and hold them, as we hold the rest of mankind, enemies that would enslave us, and enslave our friends.

I therefore, being without good and proper representation, appealing to the supreme judge of the world for the rectitude of my intentions, do, in the name and by the authority of natural law, solemnly publish and declare, that I am, and ought to be, a free and independent entity. That I am absolved from all allegiance to our modern royalty, that all political connection between myself and the statist republicrats, is and ought to be totally dissolved; and that as a free and independent voter, I have full power to join with others, vote them out of office, contract alliances, establish commerce, and to do all other things which free people may of right do.-And for the support of this declaration, with a firm self-reliance, I pledge to protect my life, my fortune, and my sacred honor.

My personal John Hancock;

S. Scott Yapp

Chapter Twenty-five

Chapter Twenty-six

Conclusion

As I started researching for this book, I had no political party affiliation. I had been a Republican, a Democrat, and an independent. The two major parties just didn't fit me. The Democrats with their insistence on social engineering by robbing from the innovators, the workers, the entrepreneurs, and giving our hard earned dollars to the non-achievers making them rely on government handouts instead of developing a work ethic, had led us down Karl Marx's path of socialism. I had not realized the extent of this because they gave their programs nice names like New Deal, Great Society, Welfare, Social Security, instead of their proper names, respectively, Bad Deal, Great Socialism, Rely on Uncle Samfare, and Ponzi-scheme Security. They claim to be for the working man, but their policies have encouraged people not to work. They have let our founding fathers down by giving out tax dollars as charity. They have expanded the federal government into the bloated and inefficient albatross it is today. They have ignored the constitutional limits on power, ignored the Tenth Amendment, and attacked capitalism at its foundation. They have protected their own members through scandal after scandal, and fleeced the public at every opportunity.

The Republicans have proven themselves to be no better. Promises to cut the size of government have been broken (cuts in growth are not reductions, who do they think they are fooling?). They have broken their word to NRA members not to let the 2nd amendment be pushed aside further. They have failed to eliminate the Department of Education. They have expanded corporate welfare, which rewards non-productive businesses and punishes the profitable and innovative businesses. They have attacked the right to privacy, freedom of speech, freedom of expression, freedom of association, all in the name of 'the good of society'. In their own way they have moved us towards a totalitarian society right along with the Democrats. They claim to be capitalists, but their tampering with the free market has proven they are not.

As I soon found out, being an independent voter had its drawbacks. Many of the 'independent' candidates weren't so independent. There are mostly no candidates on the ballot except those from the two major parties, and sometimes the incumbent is even unopposed. The independents that do run are a mixed bag of nuts. Remember Ross "the Cuban hit squads are after me" Perot?

I became convinced that the only solution was to find a third party. It had to be a party that believed in the Constitution. It had to be a party that stood up for our founding fathers ideals. One that held sacred the values of capitalism, freedom, justice, and all the things that made this country great .A party that held the values of the Christian Thomas Jefferson as well as the atheist Ayn Rand. A party that believed in the notion that the individual rights of its citizens were to be held above the socialist ideology of ' the good of society'. One that believed that the least government was the best government as Madison, Jay, Washington, Hamilton, Franklin, and all the great innovators of our revolution have believed.

As I searched the Internet for various research documents (like the Federalist Papers, and writings of Jefferson, Washington, Ayn Rand etc.), I kept seeing a party's name come up. I had heard of them before, but didn't know much about them. One evening, I followed a link to their Internet site. I was up all night looking at page after page of the writings of statesmen. This was what I was looking for. A party of principle. A party that believed in America and it's citizens.

I joined the third largest party in the US, the Libertarian Party. In the several years that have passed, I have done my part in helping to make it grow. Right now we are the fastest growing party in the US, and at times we are the only party that is growing and not losing members. We have started winning elections, and more importantly, our ideas and ideology have caught on. We are the party that has been calling for the elimination of the IRS. Now some of the 'mainstream' politicians have had this same idea! We have been for privatization of the Social Security system, and as we approach 2013 (the year the politician's cash cow runs out of milk), more and more of them will want to do the same. All across the country, private solutions have been proving themselves. From privatized school system, jails, even private money, the free market is once again proving that it has no equal.

I strongly believe that we, the Libertarians, are the best hope for America. If we fail to bring back freedom, downsize the government, and bring back statesmen, the future will be bleak. The ominous specter of a totalitarian police state that takes from all its citizens everything including hope is what drives me to work harder. We must succeed at the ballot box, for if we do not, there is a movement taking hold in the country, that I fear will not be able to be stopped.

For several years, the press has been reporting about organized militias and various other groups training and gathering weaponry. David Koresh and the Branch Dividians were one such group, but they were small and just wanted to be left alone. Many of the others are much more organized and aggressive. Tim Mcveigh tragically proved that just a few people with limited resources could wreak havoc on our society. Congress, in its infinite wisdom, instead of recognizing the root of the problem, passed more laws including one that made it more difficult for farmers to get fertilizer. What is needed to fight this domestic terrorism is more freedom, not less.

The interference in people's lives by the government is what has caused these militias to grow. People who have not initialized force should be left alone. Punishment for crimes should be swift and sure, but we must make sure that crime is defined to give the individual maximum freedom. Laws that protect us from others are necessary, but laws that protect us from ourselves only breed resentment. Consenting adults should be left alone in their behavior, even if we find that behavior offensive. This is the definition of freedom. I am not gay, but gay people should be able to live as they want, as long as they do not interfere with others rights to do the same. I am not a drug addict, but what an adult puts into his or her own body is their own business. Just don't ask me to pay for their medical expenses when they fry their brains. I have never bought the services of a prostitute, but if the adults involved are consenting, it's none of my business or anyone else's why they have sex.

There is a crucial difference in protecting us from violent criminals, from thieves, from con artists, and from those that prey on various members of our communities, and protecting us from ourselves. A violent criminal takes away someone else's rights, whether it's murder, rape, or assault, they have forcefully taken away your right to life, liberty, and the pursuit of happiness. A thief has forcefully taken away the possessions of another. A con artist has forcefully taken away your money or trust by trickery. These people need to be punished. On the other hand, who has forced anyone in a drug deal? Who's rights have been taken away by a prostitute? Who is the victim? Society can not be the victim. I am a member of this society, and in these examples, how have my rights been abridged? They have not. And as an equal member of this society, I demand that our police get the real criminals behind bars where they belong, and leave the non-criminals alone.

As technology increases, and the ability to really control all aspects of someone's life becomes available, is it wise to put so much power in the hands of so few? Or would we all be much safer and happier to govern our own lives? After much studying of their writings, I think that the founders of this great nation understood that in order for this country to survive the test of time, it must respect the rights of the individual. We can not allow the federal government to become the sole source of power in the United States. This is not what was intended, and it will lead to the destruction of all we hold sacred.

Must we gather on the green as our forefathers did in 1776

and fight again for our liberty? Do we have to revert again to taking up arms and declaring our freedom? Or can we seize the moment and use the weapon of the ballot box to vanquish those who would enslave us?

The choice is ours. Do we bring liberty back, or do we regress into anarchy? I have made my choice. Over 200 years ago, our founders were fed up with their government. They hit critical mass. What ensued was a bloody revolution that spawned the greatest nation that has ever existed. Now I am at critical mass. My explosion will be at the ballot box, and by making my voice of freedom heard by those I meet and deal with.

My only fear is that if we, the Libertarians, are not successful, that if the Marxist Republicrats win, that a great number of our people will hit critical mass, and their explosion will rock the world.

Chapter Twenty-six

Chapter Twenty-seven

Definitions

Black Market- Businesses created by the unwise banning or over-regulation of a product desired by consumers. This is a natural response of the free market, one that can not be overcome by any amount of laws. Like most government intrusions into the free market, attempts to stop certain sales like drugs and toilets has the opposite effect as intended, actually causing the entrepreneurs that deal in such items to make even more money.

Business- For-profit enterprise that provides jobs, services, and goods to the masses. Most businesses have less than 25 employees.

Capitalism- Economic System based on the premise that people own the product of their labor. Rewards those who strive to excel. Rewards and pushes forward innovation by allowing those who innovate to profit from it. Allows ownership of private property and ideas. This system made the USA a world power by its ability to produce advancements in every segment of society. No other system rewards innovation, so other systems become stagnant while capitalism flourishes.

Capitalist- Person that believes that individuals, not government, should determine the best products and ideas through their purchases. Capitalists are hated by communists since some people will make more money than others under a capitalist system. Capitalists know that by allowing the free market to sort out the economic winners and losers, that not only will better products and ideas be presented to the public, but also that the entire economy and the standard of living is elevated.

Communism- Economic-Political system that bans ownership of private property. All property and ideas belong to the community. The leaders decide what's in the community's best interest, and if that means taking your business or your wife in the name of what's best they can and will do it.

Communist- Believes that self-sacrifice is better than self-reliance. Wants no part of capitalism or profit. Believes that all men should serve others. Thinks that the only reason communism has never worked is because the right people have not been in charge.

Congress-Opposite of progress- elected body that should know better than the crap they legislate. Overpaid, oversexed, pompous, lying weasels.

Conservative- Person that believes that government should be smaller, but goes out of their way to make it larger. Does not like individual rights, but thinks large corporations and politicians should be above the law. Caters to the religious right and blames all of societies ills on perceived immorality.

Crime- Denying another person or persons of their natural rights. A crime has three essential elements; Intent, force, and a clear-cut victim. If an arrest occurs without all 3 of these elements in place, it is tyranny and should be nullified by a jurist or jury.

Criminal- Person who through direct or indirect force or coercion, denies or takes away the equal right or rights of another person or persons.

Democrat- Member of political party that claims they are the party for the common man, yet their policies show differently. They tend to be statists, and they love big government programs. They differ from socialists only slightly in that they view capitalism in a mixed economy as a necessary evil. They love social programs and tend to think that the only way to solve any problem is to throw more (tax) money at it.

Discrimination- Favoring one group of individuals over another based on physical characteristics or ancestry. Can not occur on a widespread level without the force of law being used to facilitate it.

Entrepreneur- Risk taker in a free market that seizes upon an idea for creating wealth, and acts upon it. As many have shown, it takes very little cash, but a lot of drive to become a successful entrepreneur.

Equality- Equality in America means equal opportunity. This goes hand in hand with liberty and capitalism. Equality does not mean equal results. This is how Marxism would have you define it, but there can not be equal results even in communism. For example, compare the living standards of Politburo members in relation to the common people of Russia.

Feudalism- System in which royalty owns all in its domain. They decide what's best. Differs from communism only slightly in that the ranks of royalty are replenished by heredity only.

Freedom- Greatly misunderstood term that means simply that an individual has control over their own life, body, mind, home, and possessions.

Government- The force of law. In America, the government is supposed to derive its power from the people, not the opposite as it is elsewhere. The government does not give us our rights, they are already ours. It is only there to protect our rights.

Innovator- Person or company that finds a better way of doing something. Innovators will usually profit from their innovations, and they will create wealth for all associated with them. They are the keys to capitalism's success, and the reason the free market can not be stopped.

Justice- The application of legal force to protect, compensate, or retaliate on behalf of a victim or victims, against a perpetrator or perpetrators.

'Laissez-faire' Capitalism-'Hands-off' capitalism means the government does not interfere with business. In a true laissez-faire capitalism, the market forces businesses to have to compete for business and employees. There is no need for a minimum wage since businesses on equal terms must compete for the best workers. The government stays out of financial affairs of private industry by neither mandating nor subsidizing. Under this system there are no long-term recessions since there are no government policies to cause them.

Law- Can be defined in one word; force. Laws are important to protect us from others who would prey on us; they should never attempt to protect us from ourselves. This is the essence of liberty.

Leader- One who holds and uses the force of law. A leader by nature wishes power, and many of them wish to enslave the rest of us. It is democracy's hope that by allowing us to choose our leaders that we will choose wisely. But alas, they do deceive us. It is my contention that a strong third party would wake and shake them up.

Legalspeak- Weasely lawyer language meant to complicate

any legal matter to the point where you need another weasel to understand it. For example, the sentence *The quick brown fox jumped the fence* becomes *The first party knowingly being fast, has therefore and hitherto extended its mass upward and forward, and therefore encroached the party of the second's perimeter barrier.*

Legislate- Force. The act of forcing ones will upon others using the force of law. Necessary when used properly, but usually used to bring tyranny upon the people.

Liberal- Person who believes that the government should operate the economy. The differences between a liberal and a socialist are in name and cosmetics only. Neither believe in a free market, and would rather use Marxist means to regulate business. Liberals claim to be pro freedom of speech, but then <u>force</u> the rest of us to fund pornographic art, or pay for close captioning for the Jerry Springer show.

Libertarianism- Philosophy based on the writings of Aristotle, George Washington, Thomas Jefferson, Ayn Rand, and others that rightfully state the peoples rights to liberty and freedom. Libertarians do not believe in the initiation of force. Force should only be used as retaliation or prevention of the initiation of force. They believe that people who have not initiated force should be left alone, that an action is only a crime if it denies the rights of someone else. They are avid capitalists believing that all men should keep the fruits of their labor, and should not be forced at gunpoint to give it to others. It differs from all other philosophies by standing up for individual rights and calling for less government intrusion into all facets of life. They believe that by rewarding innovation and the achievers, more people desire to innovate and achieve, thus moving technology, society, and the economy along at a quicker pace creating a higher standard of living for all people.

Liberty- The natural right of an individual to exercise their own freewill while regarding the equal rights of others to do the same.

Lobbyist- Person who tries to influence our leaders by legal and illegal means. From sex, to money, to trips to the Caribbean, they have used all available means to undermine our liberty.

Looting- Using the cover of law to steal. Some looters steal during riots, others call themselves lawyers and extort money out of companies like Philip Morris and Microsoft. Ayn Rand warned in *The Atlas Shrugged* of government looters.

Mixed economy- Economy that mixes Capitalism with Socialism. Supporters of socialism try to wipe away capitalism by looting, promising voters a free lunch (chicken in every pot, Social Security, Great Society, etc…), and by outright lies. They object to profits, and hate innovators who do profit as in the case of Bill Gates.

Moderate- Wide open term generally referring to swing

voters, that is, people who are not ideologically bound to one party or the other. It is very easy to be moderate, since both major parties have little ideological honesty.

Monopoly- A business or government entity that *completely* controls a sector of the economy. These are rare, and can not occur without help from the force of law (government). The free market will not create monopolies, only control of the market by the force of government can create them. The term monopoly should never be used without the word coercive preceding it.

Morality- An individual's code of ethics, based on their own religion and philosophy. Morality can not be forced on another, since it is part of each person's own mind and soul.

Natural Rights- Those rights which we are born with. God-given rights. Rights that no man or group of men should ever take away. Our country was formed on the premise of natural rights.

Politician- One who makes many promises in order to become a leader, breaks many promises after becoming a leader, and uses the force of law to perpetuate themselves as leaders.

Politics- The manner in which our modern masters have kept us enslaved. By constant grandstanding on the minor points of law and non-issues, they have diverted attention from their illegal and unconstitutional power grab. (Read the Tenth Amendment again.)

Pork- Public or private projects that are paybacks for political support that are funded by hard earned tax money, taken by force from citizens.

Porkbarrel- Feeding trough of our modern masters, where they pay each other back for support. This absolutely unconstitutional practice costs us billions every year.

Privatize- To dismantle big or small wasteful government programs, and let the free market handle them. To make a wasteful and unprofitable taxpayer funded operation more efficient by turning it over to the private sector, where it should have been to begin with.

Racism- Hatred and discrimination against any group of individuals based on their ancestry or physical characteristics.

Republican- Member of political party that tends to look out for the interests of business and wealth. Republicans miss the mark on most individual rights issues. Some Republicans however are much more like libertarians and should instead consider the Libertarian Party. In recent years, Republicans have pushed in corporate welfare, and went along with the Democrats on a great many issues. They have also abandoned their traditional NRA constituents, and that along with other mistakes has cost the party the momentum that they seemed to have in the 80's and the early 90's. They are very quickly making themselves obsolete.

Religion- Ones own personal beliefs on God or the afterlife.

Some use religion as a substitute for philosophy, others use it as a club to beat their fellow man with. Our forefathers knew this, and wisely put a wall of separation between religion and government.

Social Security- Racist Ponzi scheme tax and spend plan that takes money from workers of all walks of life and gives it primarily to white retirees. Supporters want you to believe that they know best how to invest your money for you and they don't trust you to save for yourself. In reality the money is not being 'saved' but spent on other things as fast as your SSI taxes are taken out of your check. Many of us will never get a dime back, and the actuary tables show that it's really a bad deal for minorities and lower income people.

Socialism- Economic System in which all belongs to 'society'. Even though most socialist countries allow private ownership of land and business, the leaders can micromanage both. Any profits can be looted from companies by the government through laws that target their industries. Factories, businesses, and land are viewed as community resources and can be destroyed, altered or stolen from their owners in the name of 'the good of society'.

Socialist- Statist. Person who believes we should all be a slave of the state and work only for the benefit of others. Most socialists lie to themselves and the rest of us and call themselves Democrats or Republicans.

Statist- Person who believes that the government should be omnipotent or all-powerful. They see the individual as a slave of the government and having few if any rights.

Subsidy- Unwise, unconstitutional tampering of the free market by government.

Tax- Taking money by force from an individual or business to pay for the activities of the government. It is crucial to understand that tax is force, and that politicians should not use this money on their own personal agendas, but rather should use it for prudent, constitutional, and necessary functions of government.

Treason- Planning to, or acting to enslave your fellow countrymen. Many of our so-called leaders are guilty of this.

Tyrant- Person who would impose their own will or morality on another.

Unalienable Right- Right that is God-given or natural. It is a right that can not be taken away by others. If they try to take an unalienable right away, man has the instinct, and yes the natural right to rebel against the tyranny which attempts to suppress this right.

Unconstitutional- Any law, regulation, public policy, or any other term for act of control that the weasels can come up with that is not <u>specifically allowed</u> by the Constitution of the United States.

User fee- Type of tax in which the actual beneficiary of the associated government program pays for it. Some good examples are the gasoline tax monies being used to develop and maintain roads, postage stamps, national park camping and sightseeing fees, alcohol and tobacco taxes, and taxes on specific products. These taxes are not only constitutional, they also are very wise since the actual user of the service pays for it without forcefully taking money from those who do not use the particular service.

Waste- Spending which is either unnecessary or unconstitutional.

Chapter Twenty-seven

Chapter Twenty-eight

Acknowledgements

The following people, in no particular order, have all had a profound effect on my life, and my philosophy. Therefore I must acknowledge their genius and help.

Ayn Rand- Author of some of the greatest books ever written including *Anthem* and *The Atlas Shrugged.*

Thomas Jefferson -Inventor, innovator, and the founding philosopher of this great nation. Author of the most eloquent *Declaration of Independence.*

Bill Gates- For proving that it's still possible to start with nothing, build the better 'mousetrap', and become the richest man in history.

Neil Peart, Geddy Lee, and Alex Lifeson- For the beauty of the music of the rock band Rush, and for leading me to the genius of Ayn Rand.

Jon Oliva and Paul O'Neil- For the wonderful symphonic sounds of Savatage and the Trans-Siberian Orchestra, and especially the inspiring story told on *Dead Winter Dead.*

James Madison- For writing the greatest of documents, the *Constitution.*

John Jay, George Washington, Ben Franklin, Thomas Paine, George Mason, and all of the founders- For risking and in some cases giving everything for liberty.

Ron Paul- For showing me that there are some good politicians, and that it's not too late for liberty.

My wife and family- For putting up with a damned libertarian.

In addition to my study of the *Constitution*, and *The Federalist Papers*, I must also acknowledge as reference materials; Adam Smith's *The Wealth of Nations*, Martin Gross's *Government Waste from A to Z*, the excellent documentary film *Waco; The Rules of Engagement*, and assorted writings of Alan Greenspan, Milton Friedman, Davy Crockett, and Harry Browne.

I would also like to thank the industrialist and inventor John Galt. His example should be a beacon of liberty in all of our hearts and minds forever.

About the Author

Critical Mass: Life, Liberty and the Pursuit of Better Government is the first book by author S. Scott Yapp. It culminates several years of studying the documents of America's Founding.

Coming soon from S. Scott Yapp

In a post-apocalyptic America completely devastated by a natural disaster, could ideals like freedom, liberty, and capitalism still survive? Author S Scott Yapp poses this question in the intense sci-fi thriller *The Shift*.

The story begins with a life-ending natural disaster of epic proportions. After years of desolation, from out of the wastelands, from deep underground, there comes the most unlikely of heroes; Edward Trask. Plagued by isolation and visited by visions of disaster, the unwilling hero gets violently swept into the growing tide of socialism. Could this one solitary man be the hope to keep the dream of a free America alive? From the front cover to the back the author weaves an unforgettably timeless story of survival and the continuing battle for freedom that every generation must endure. *The Shift* is a must read for all lovers of liberty and science fiction alike.

www.ingramcontent.com/pod-product-compliance
Lightning Source LLC
Chambersburg PA
CBHW060850280326
41934CB00007B/991